To Tilt at Windmills

Fred Thomas, 1986

To Tilt at Windmills

Windmills

A MEMOIR OF THE SPANISH CIVIL WAR

Fred Thomas

The British Anti-Tank Battery
The Fifteenth International Brigade

Michigan State University Press

East Lansing

All Michigan State University Press books are produced on paper which meets the requirements of American National Standard of Information Science—Permanence of paper for printed materials ANSI Z39.48-1984.

Michigan State University Press
East Lansing, Michigan 48823-5202

03 02 01 00 99 98 97 96 1 2 3 4 5 6 7 8 9

Library of Congress Cataloging-in-Publication Data

Thomas, Fred A.

To tilt at windmills ; a memoir of the Spanish Civil War / Fred A. Thomas.
        p.   cm.
    Includes index.
    ISBN 0-87013-421-3
    1. Spain—Histoty—Civil War, 1936-1938—Personal narratives, British.
    2. Thomas, Fred A. 3. Spain—Histoty—Civil War, 1936-1938—Campaigns.
    4. Spain—Histoty—Civil War, 1936-1938—Participation, British. 5. British—Spain—
History—20th century. 6. Spain Ejército Popular de la Républica. Brigada
Internacional, XV—Bibliography. I. Title.
DP269.9.T52   1996
946.08—dc20   96-16939
                                                              CIP

This book is for:

All those in the International Brigades and the many others who did what they could to help the Spanish people; Jose (Pepe) Lopez, a dear departed friend; and Sadie, in the hope that it helps to ease the pain of the loss of her brother, Max Nash, lying unmarked, unknown, somewhere in Ebro.

CONTENTS

Preface

When Spain's Second Republic was challenged by a military uprising on 18 July 1936, the Civil War which ensued developed into the most savage battle of a European class war which had smouldered sporadically since the Russian revolution of 1917. Immediately after the First World War, revolutionary outbreaks were brutally suppressed in Germany and Hungary. The organized left was dismantled in Italy by Mussolini's fascists and in Spain and Portugal by conservative dictatorships. The triumph of nazism in Germany in 1933 was the prelude to the destruction of the world's most powerful working class movement. In February 1934, the Austrian left was defeated by Dollfuss. France was bitterly divided between left and a broad array of ultra-rightist and fascist groupings. Even in relatively stable Britain, the bitterness which followed the defeat of the General Strike in 1926 and the social costs of the Great Depression intensified social divisions. By late 1932, Oswald Moseley's black-shirted British Union of Fascists were stalking the East End of London in search of Jewish victims. In Britain, as in France, only the Communist Party mounted serious opposition to the spread of Fascism.

Accordingly, when the Spanish Civil War broke out, the Comintern took advantage of the spontaneous left-wing movement across non-fascist Europe in support of the Second Republic to organize the International Brigades from mid-August. Italian, German, and Austrian refugees from Nazism saw the Spanish Civil War as their first chance to fight back against the fascism which had forced them from their homelands. Some were out-of-work, a few were adventurers, but the majority had a clear idea of why they had come. French (the most numerous contingent), British, and North American volunteers went to Spain out of concern about what defeat for the Republic might mean in terms of the spread of fascism in the rest of the world. Volunteers traveled via Paris

ix

thence to be smuggled through mountain paths across the Franco-Spanish border or in fishing boats to the Basque coast. The first arrived in Spain in October. They were given a minimum of primitive basic training at the International Brigade Headquarters established at Albacete.

On 8 November, the first units reached a Madrid at the mercy of General Franco's advancing armies. They were made up of German and Italian anti-fascists, together with some British, French, and Polish left-wingers, a few of whom had fought in the First World War or had some other experience of military service. Their arrival was vital to the heroic popular effort that made up the defense of the capital. Sprinkled among the Spanish defenders at the rate of one to four, they were not only able to pass on their expertise to the civilians, but their solidarity also had an incalculable impact in terms of boosting the morale of the Madrileños. Thereafter, led by the Soviet General Émil Kléber, the International Brigades played a decisive part in repelling efforts by the Nationalists to encircle Madrid. Casualties among the International Brigades were especially numerous. This was hardly surprising given the disparity in training and equipment enjoyed by Franco's hardened colonial army. In February, the rebels attacked through the Jarama valley on the Madrid-Valencia highway to the East of the capital. Fiercely defended, the road was held at a cost of 25,000 Republicans including some of the best British and American members of the Brigades.

In March, further Nationalist efforts to encircle Madrid by attacking Guadalajara were defeated by a counter-attack involving the Italian Garibaldi Battalion of the International Brigades, Thereafter, as the Republic organized its Popular Army, and as the conflict turned into a war of large-scale conventional armies, the brigades played an important but less central role.

The Brigades played a significant role in later offensives mounted by the Republican Chief of Staff General Vicente Rojo—in the bloody stalemate at Brunete, near Madrid in July 1937, in the capture of Belchite near Zaragoza in August 1937, that of Teruel in January 1938, and in the final defensive phase of the war. This followed Franco's great offensive through the spring and summer of 1938 after his recapture of Teruel in February 1938. Sweeping through Aragón and Castellón, 100,000 Nationalist troops reached the Mediterranean by mid-April splitting Republican Spain in two. In July, Franco's armies moved toward Valencia. Republican forces, including the Brigades, mounted a determined defense. Then, to relieve the threat against Valencia, the Republic mounted a daring assault across the River Ebro in an attempt to restore contact with Catalonia. The Nationalist lines were breached, although at great cost to the Brigades. Francoist reinforcements were rushed in. After sustaining three months of relentless air attack and artillery bombardment in suffocating heat, the Republicans were pushed back.

It was essentially the end for the Republic. In the vain hope of securing international support, the Republic unilaterally withdrew the volunteers. A formal farewell parade was held in Barcelona for them at the end of October 1938. They had fought and suffered for an ideal, without expectation of reward, and now faced an at best uncertain future. It is impossible to calculate the military impact of the International Brigades on the survival of the Spanish Republic, Suffice it to say that, from the siege of Madrid through Jarama, Guadalajara, Brunete, and Teruel, to the final inferno of the Ebro, it was an immense contribution. Although the Republic was ultimately defeated, the scale of its resistance dramatically diminished Mussolini's military capability in 1940. The duration of the Republican war effort delayed Hitler's ultimate attack on France and, in a sense, gave Britain more time in which to rearm.

The story of the International Brigades just briefly recounted has given rise to a substantial bibliography and a rich collection of autobiographical material. From the end of the Spanish war in April 1939, the challenge facing any International Brigade veteran contemplating writing memoirs was to capture both the political elation of the early days of the war and the desperate tragedy of the Republic's demise. There have been memoirs which admirably evoke the romantic spirit of the early volunteers and others, most notably Jason Guerney's *Crusade in Spain,* which convey the disillusion of defeat. One of the many merits of Fred Thomas' memoir is that without ever striking a false note, he manages to recreate both the grandeur and the misery that was the experience of the volunteers.

Written in an entirely unheroic, not to say, self-deprecating manner, this book is both a fitting tribute to the self-sacrifice and human solidarity of the International Brigades and an important contribution to the military history of the war. Fred Thomas was, in 1936, a Labour party militant from Hackney in the East End of London, deeply outraged by the anti-Semitic activities of Mosley's Black Shirts. His account of how his anti-fascism in London led him to give up his job and undertake the hazardous journey to Spain is a valuable contribution to the historiography of the

Brigades. However, what gives *To Tilt at Windmills* its unique atmosphere and its value to historians of the Spanish Civil War is the fact that, unlike most of its predecessors, it is based on a carefully kept diary.

It is a tribute to the author, and to his diary, that the book is painfully honest throughout, although regularly tinged with an engaging humour. That honesty is the antithesis of the literary artifice which has crept into the memoirs of some of his predecessors. The book is in the form of the diary together with a commentary both in terms of his present memory of events and an emotional return visit to Spain with fellow veterans in 1981. Fred Thomas is not afraid to say occasionally that he simply cannot remember things that he wrote at the time. He is self-critical—about the naiveté of his early entries and the moaning and grumbling of his Teruel phase—just as he is gently scathing about the apparent total recall of other memoir writers. Although much of what he recounts is admirable and heroic, he recounts his participation in the most matter-of-fact, yet vivid way. In this regard, it is worth noting his description of the naïve pleasure that he and his comrades derived from their first training on newish Russian anti-tank guns: "This was great fun. We were playing at soldiers in the pleasantest way possible, with no enemy to answer back." With similar frankness, he talks of the volunteers' "abysmal ignorance" of Spanish politics and the internecine struggles taking place between anarchists, Trotskyists, Socialists, and Stalinists. As he says: "anything not immediately and obviously affecting our daily lives—bitter cold or searing heat, hunger or thirst, mail, and ciga-rettes—seemed remote and unreal."

The enormous value of the foundation of the detailed diary is that much of what he says can be followed with a map and collated with many of the extant military histories of the war and of particular battles. It thus provides an invaluable source for military historians. Like the best memoirs, it is excellent on atmosphere but, unlike them, does not confine description of activities to generalities in which villages, valleys, and actions are difficult to locate in time or place. There is no battle in which he took part that is not illuminated by his "worm's eye view."

On the Jarama front, which he reached after the worst of the fighting was over, his first impression of its labyrinth of lines, communicating trenches, and dugouts was: "God knows how men stood four years of this in the Great War, in which they had no real interest. It is an incredibly stupid, filthy, primitive, barbaric business." He provides an intensely revealing description of the chaos of the Republican offensive at Brunete in July 1937, vividly showing the consequences for the men on the ground of Nationalist air and artillery superiority. Curiously, he arrives at the conclusion that, although Brunete is usually considered to have been a victory for Franco in terms of the attrition balance, the fact of being able to mount an offensive at all was a great morale booster for the Republican troops.

The horrors of the Teruel campaign are equally well evoked with an ironic touch as he describes freezing in an open truck on New Year's Eve 1937. Again the intense awareness of the overwhelming superiority of Franco's artillery and aircraft, and of the poor military technique of the Republican command, helps explain how initial Republican triumph was gradually turned into defeat. Perhaps most valuable of all is his lengthy description of his unit's part in the battle of the Ebro. With great freshness, he recreates the mood of optimism of the early Ebro attack and shows how the appalling conditions, bridges breaking, the insufficiency of the arms and equipment transported across the river, the heat, the water shortages, the relentless bombing, machine gunning, and artillery bombardments turned that mood into one of despair. Fred Thomas has produced the best account in English of the battle as seen from the ground as against the accounts from the comfort of the command posts.

Alongside this invaluable contribution to the military history of the Spanish Civil War, Fred Thomas has added significantly to the literature of popular history. In this regard, the book is full of brilliant perceptions and sharply observed details, whether it be moving scenes of children begging for scraps in besieged Madrid, or his observations in Barcelona, on his return from hospitalization after being wounded, of the barracks in which he was billeted. Demoralized men with no mattresses, no blankets, and appalling food which had to be eaten from old tins and jam jars itched to get back to the front while smartly uniformed, well-equipped soldiers walk around the Ramblas with pretty girls on their arms.

The Spanish Civil War is a story of cruelty and brutality but also one of the most inspiring human solidarity. It is a story which consists of many thousands of published versions and hundreds of thousands of accounts that will never see the light of day. Its capacity to move and to appall is hardly diminished nearly sixty years after its outbreak. Without pretense or falsity, with warmth, directness and a deep humanity, Fred Thomas has added an important contribution to the collective memory of the war.

Paul Preston
London School of Economics

Acknowledgements

It is customary for authors to thank those who have assisted him. I must first make very clear my debt to one without whose vigorous help my book would probably still be going the rounds of unappreciative British publishers. Professor Victor Howard of Michigan State University first read my manuscript five years ago and very gratifyingly saw sufficient merit in it to speak of possible publication by his own university press. A mild form of masochism caused me to persist for four years more in suffering self-inflicted wounds via publishers' letters regretting their inability to see much profit to themselves from publication. It was the pleasant intervention of another Yank, Saul Wellman, a comrade in the International Brigade, who provided the encouragement which finally gave Professor Howard his chance to work so hard and to such purpose that *To Tilt At Windmills* is at last in print. To him I offer my thanks and gratitude.

Thanks also to Jenny Hayes who first turned an almost illegible scrawl into a typescript and who expressed her admiration for the work—the first and much needed praise. Thanks also to Claire Tomalin and Martyn Harris for their good opinions. And thanks to those friends who blatantly showed bias which, if recognised as such, still gave much pleasure.

Thanks to Professor Paul Preston who took time from his already over-laden work schedule to prepare the Preface.

Finally, thanks to Sadie, my wife, who has suffered many hours of neglect without too much complaint!

Acknowlegement is made to the Marx Memorial Library in London for the use of photographs. The Center for Cartographic Research and Spacial Analysis at Michigan State University for preparing the maps. And the staff of the Michigan State University Press, in particular Kristen Lare, Julie Loehr, and Michael Brooks have been of great assistance.

I

May-June 1937
From Hackney to the Jarama Front

Go proudly. You are history, you are legend. We shall not forget you, and
when the olive tree of peace puts forth its leaves again, mingled with the lau-
rels of the Spanish Republic's victory—come back.

— Dolores Ibarruri—"La Pasionaria"

The Farewell Parade to the International Brigades,

Barcelona, 28 October 1938

A plane touched down at Madrid Airport in the evening of 30th April
1981. Forty-two of the hundred or so passengers shared a common excitement. Some old, all at least elderly, we might have been on a Saga package
tour somewhat off course for one of Spain's warmer resorts. We were in
fact all veterans of the International Brigade, a fast diminishing band who
went from many countries to fight on the side of the Republican government in the Spanish Civil War of 1936-1939. Now, some of the few who
remain, we had come from Britain to see again those places so very special
to us in our memories. At last we had come back. No red carpet greeted
us, though filming our arrival was a television crew of the BBC. So indelibly has the Civil War made its mark upon history that the BBC had decided
we were to be accompanied as we went, second time around, to the battlefields.

To be in Madrid again was an emotional experience not easily
described. For many of the earliest volunteers who had fought in or for the
city or, like myself, been fortunate enough to get a few days' leave there,
poignant memories were brought vividly to the surface. From the airport
we had driven past the Palace Hotel, long since returned to its Five Star
opulence, but in whose room 406 I passed a few painful days after being
wounded at Brunete in 1937.

1

Then I saw the Hotel Nacional and recalled a wonderful week on leave in November 1937.

In the chill sunshine of that long gone winter, flags and banners fluttered from buildings in proud defiance, celebrating the city's first anniversary of resistance to Franco. The government had removed to Valencia, but it was here that the spirit of the Republic lived. Madrid was a city of proclamations. Every wall carried exhortations to the people of Madrid—of Spain—to resist and conquer. And everywhere it seemed to me this determination to defeat fascism was evident in the looks and bearing of the citizens, hunger, cold, and even death notwithstanding. Franco's forces had been stopped at the city's edge by the courage and sacrifice of Spaniards and Internationals. Madrileños had won their precious freedom from church and state and landlords through the ballot box, and now were defending it with rifles and their lives. Several churches gutted and black from fire and smoke told their own grim tale of the people's need to strike back. When had the Church stood up for them? On whose side was it now? Bishops and Archbishops of the Catholic Church were regularly blessing the arms of Franco's soldiers in their "Christian Crusade."

Frustrated in his attempts to capture the nation's capital, Franco bombed and shelled the city haphazardly in a futile endeavour to break the defenders' spirit. If anything, it added to their resolve; hate is a powerful stimulant. By and large, Madrileños learnt to endure these evidences of Franco's goodwill with a stoicism to be emulated later by the people of so many of our own cities. In the Gran Via they tried to keep to one side of the road. Away from the city center, yet so frighteningly near, manned barricades and strong points barred the way. Beyond was the University City and the Casa de Campo, Madrid's front line.

In my diary of those days, assiduously kept and carefully guarded for the whole of my twenty months in Spain, I wrote:

November 5th. 1937. Towards the University City and the Casa de Campo the bustle and life of the city changes, giving way more and more to a sense of desolation, emptiness and destruction. Here is where the fighting of a year ago and much shelling since have taken most toll. Here Madrid still stands a hairsbreadth from disaster.

To-day, Nils Kruth, my American friend, and I hired a horse—or rather a mule-cab to take us around for a few hours. It was a small open carriage, about as rare as in London, which is strange when you think what a large part mules play in general transport here. Strings of them, laden with good-ness knows what, are a common sight in the streets. Anyway, Kruth and I sat up in style like a couple of pocket generals, much to the amusement of the onlookers. From several feet above ground level we saw a good deal of Madrid in comfort. There was never any danger of going too fast for as our driver was at pains to point out, the mule didn't get enough food for that! We asked him to take us as near to University City as he was allowed but whether he was nervous for his mule, himself, or us I don't know for the more we urged him on, barricades and other hindrances permitting, the more reluctant he became. Incidentally it was interesting to note how the Government has taken the trouble to brick up all kinds of monuments and statues for their protection from shelling and bombs. I thought we were all supposed to be barbarians.

At night in the blacked-out streets we used to stand and stare into the darkness, watching for the occasional flash and waiting for the crack of rifle fire from the trenches. Then we would turn and join the jostling queue to gain a table in the rare hotel which received a food ration of sorts for such as we. Inside, the expensive furnishings and general decor, the tableware, the hanging chandeliers (one bulb in fifty shedding light now) the hovering waiters—some of whom we were convinced took a very poor view of their current patrons—contrasted starkly with the dark, ominous reality outside and, too, with the bean soup augmented on good nights by a chunk of bread which made up the meal, and for which colonels and privates, haughty señoras and señores pushed and shoved to win a place. When available the bread was issued as we entered the restau-rant and clutched grimly in the ensuing scramble for seats. On two nights of our five it was all we did get.

Walking breakfastless one morning in the Puerta del Sol, Kruth and I sat down at a café table and were served small cups of black, synthetic, sugarless coffee. Then to our surprise we were each given a saucer of what, on close inspection, we decided were raw sardines, or something very like them, very small and with scraps of tomato, and all floating in olive oil. Almost at once, as London sparrows alight at the feet of a sand-wich eater, several small children were at our side. Ill-dressed, pathetic, they pleaded in soft, low voices, looking directly at us with large, round eyes. Shouting threats, the waiter drove them off. Despondent, they retreated, except for two, a boy and girl perhaps 9 or 10 years old. Hungrier or bolder than their fellows, these two ventured again. Neither

Kruth nor I had done more than taste the unappetizing dish before us. Silently, we motioned to the children. At once they were at our table and within seconds the small portions were eaten. With hasty, "Gracias señores," they were off. Swallowing the dregs of our coffee we agreed our sacrifice was slight—all that olive oil!

Grimy, disheveled soldiers trudged back from the front line, going to their homes for a few hours leave. For the people of Madrid there was death and suffering, cold and hunger and disease; yet all seemed in accord with the huge posters showing a stern-faced young soldier grasping his rifle with, by his side, a young woman in factory overalls: "Venceremos!" it proclaimed—"We shall conquer."

One afternoon during those memorable six days' leave, I went on my own to a theatre. There were no shows in the evenings. Every turn was enthusiastically applauded by the audience, a motley throng of soldiers and civilians, whole families, babies included. My Spanish was inadequate to catch more than a smattering, but the obvious comic told a joke which sent the entire house into a gale of laughter followed by wild shouting and cheers. I labored to obtain a translation:

> God was worried about the state of the world and sent Saint Peter down on a tour of inspection. He reported back on the affairs of a number of capital cities.
> But what of Madrid? asked God.
> No idea, replied Peter, the anti-aircraft guns kept me out!

Now, with some of my comrades from those days, I would walk Madrid's streets once more. That night our party went to bed very late. There was so much to talk about, so many memories. Even so, when finally we dispersed to our rooms I was still too excited to sleep. The years fell away, back to the troubled thirties, and my journey from England to join the International Brigade.

It is easy now to recognize the unbroken but twisted chain of events that led, eventually, to my finding myself in Spain's Civil War. Nobody cajoled, coerced or bullied me into making the decision; certainly not the Communist Party, even though, at my request, they provided the means. It was no easy decision reached on impulse. Indeed, I hesitated longer, perhaps much longer, than a good anti-fascist ought in the face of such a threat to all a young socialist stood for.

Since 1931 I had been an active member of the Hackney Labour Party in northeast London. Soon came Hitler's traumatic rise to power and the rapid, brutal, suppression of democracy and freedom in Germany. In Britain Mosley formed his British Union of Fascists and, apeing his master, turned his thugs loose on Jews and all who opposed him.[1] But there was no clarion call from Labour to the people of Britain to get out on the streets and fight this evil of fascism.[2] It was to the communists that we had to look for leadership. "Anti-fascist Committees" were formed in almost every London borough, usually led or inspired by communists but supported by local Labour party people, liberals, churchmen and, of course, Jews. (Though the Jewish hierarchy seemed as reluctant to come out fighting as was the Labour Party). I was soon busy, speaking at meetings, adding my presence and voice to the vociferous opposition at fascist street-corner speakers. It was, frequently, a frightening and testing experience; Mosley's louts had been well drilled in the use of fists, boots and belts. Only once at Ridley Road, a favorite fascist meeting place, did I see the police act. Then, it was not to warn the speaker for making the customary obscene, ignorant, and certainly provocative attacks on Jews, but to pull out "troublemakers" from the crowd. I was one.

Many people have found it convenient to say we were used by the comrades. The truth is that their energy and initiative played a major part in rallying many thousands to show their detestation of Mosley and his mindless ones. At its very lowest evaluation, this surge of popular feeling countered the inclination of some important people (including at least one newspaper owner and more than one prominent leader of the Labour Party) to see in Mosley their looked-for strong man who would recognize their right to power and privilege.

So, politics then was a simple matter of being anti-fascist or fascist. Never has there been in England an issue creating such intense emotional fervor. When Franco and his Moors began their revolt in Spain in July 1936, at once it seemed everything crystallized into a glaringly simple truth. Fascism must be halted.

The situation in Spain called for every one of us who opposed fascism to do his utmost to defeat it. Meetings, demonstrations, collecting food, money, medical supplies, seemed no longer the answer. I determined to go to Spain myself. I had no wish for heroism, nor did I think Spain would live or die on my decision: I just knew I had to go.

In truth, I think emotion rather than cold reasoning determined the moment of decision. In the *Daily Express* I saw a picture of Franco's troops entering a captured village. Distraught women ran forward, arms outstretched in hopeless submission, pleading for the lives of their men. I could not bear the anguish in their eyes. Somewhere else, in another photo, a line of young militiamen, roped together, defeated, abject, were being marched off to immediate execution. I was obsessed by hate for the arrogant, swaggering Civil Guard officer, pistol in hand, at their head. Almost daily I read of massacres of men and women shot down in cold blood. The bombing of Guernica followed, near the end of April. And, unexpectedly, Galsworthy! When and why he wrote these lines I do not know, but they struck an answering chord in me:

> Come, let us lay a lance in rest,
> And tilt at windmills under a wild sky;
> For who could live so petty and unblest
> That dare not tilt at something ere he die
> Rather than, screened by safe majority,
> preserve his little life to little ends
> And never raise a rebel cry.[3]

In April 1937 I made my first approach. The only way I knew of was through the Communist Party, so I phoned their head office in King Street, London. Understandably, whomever I spoke to was scathing; did I really think such matters were discussed on the phone? I took a half day off from work and called there.

I've no idea whom I saw that first time, but he obviously shared my own view that the survival of the Spanish Republic did not depend on my prompt arrival. Had I any military experience or training? I assured him I had been on the streets doing my bit in the struggle against Mosley. That smart answer brought a short, sharp lecture. The Spanish people were engaged in a life or death struggle, there was no place for any except trained men. At the time I felt fittingly rebuked. Later, when I had been in Spain long enough to get my bearings, I sometimes wondered about the strange "training" some of the veterans had received!

Daily the news from Spain became more alarming. Aided by the farce of Nonintervention, Franco's troops were advancing steadily, capturing town after town, whole provinces.[4] Maps made depressing viewing, with considerably more than half the country in fascist occupation. Since November 1936 they had been at the very gates of Madrid; in the North, the Basque country was cut off, its troops being inexorably driven back. Seeking crumbs of comfort where we could we delighted in press reports—glamourized, dramatised, and largely inaccurate—of such exploits as those of "Potato Jones," captain of a British merchant ship who, we read, had successfully defied the blockading insurgent warships to land much-needed food for the people of Bilbao.[5] In London and elsewhere hundreds of children, refugees from bombs and starvation, were arriving to be cared for by a wide variety of kindly organizations and individuals.[6]

I decided to try again. This time, another interviewer and a very different response. Rightly, he was inquisitive and guarded. Why did I want to go to Spain? Was I in the Communist Party? Was I in work? Was I married? Was there anyone who would vouch for me? I muddled through with platitudes, facts, and the name of a Hackney C.P. member whom I knew well. Then—"Come back on Thursday. Till then, keep your mouth shut!"

This seemed more like it. Something told me I was as good as on my way. On Thursday I was back at King Street. The Party man was brief and to the point. Apparently my contact had reported favourably and they obviously liked the fact that I was unmarried and in work. Anyway, I was accepted.[7]

Report here on Saturday morning, 10oc. You'll be given final instructions then. Remember, you still say nothing to anyone.

How different everything and everybody seemed as I stepped out into the street again. I think I remained in a haze of unreality until I found myself actually in Spain.

I made some few essential arrangements, being compelled in the process to let three or four people know my plans. On Saturday morning, I went back to King Street for a final briefing. It was more final than I had expected. A small party of volunteers was to go that same night! Plenty of time, though, for me to settle some remaining, personal matters and make my farewells. Plenty of time—except that the Transport and General Workers' Union, in a very uncomradely gesture, had called a public transport strike for that day, 1 May 1937. I gave myself a rare treat and returned to Hackney by taxi.

For several years I had been a keen cyclist. My particular pal, a fellow member of a famous cycling club (colors and politics both very blue)

arrived that afternoon in his newly acquired car intent on a jaunt. Instead
he found he was to take me to Victoria Station. He told me I was a bloody
fool but of course did not refuse this last service. At the station entrance
we shook hands and parted. Then I rang the friends with whom I had
been living and said my final goodbyes.

Dressed in my best "plus-fours" I boarded the boat train, carrying only
the very small case King Street had recommended. Officially we were off
to Paris for the weekend so there were no passport problems. My ticket
(about £2.50 I think) had been given to me that morning. I can remember
only two of our group, George Baker, from Tonypandy, and Tony
McClean, the group leader, the only one with information as to what we
were to do when we reached Dunquerque; a variety of routes were used
to allay suspicion. There was much cloak and dagger work already afoot,
for we had been warned not to stay together, or even show we knew each
other. Going to Spain to join up was illegal: inciting others to do so even
more serious.[8] Rightly, the Communist Party wished to protect itself as
well as us.

I was nervous—not at the thought of Spain and all its alarms, but the
more immediately frightening possibility was that I might lose McClean.
Until then, sixpenny boat trips from Brighton Beach had been the limit of
my seagoing. However, since the train ran straight on to the boat, all was
well for awhile. If, as we had been warned, Special Branch were on the
lookout for such as we, then the watcher must have had some fun. We
made such a point of not being observed when we were, separately,
checking the exact whereabouts of the others that we might as well have
stayed in a bunch. There had been a France-England match that day,
rugby, I think, and the returning Frenchmen kept up a lively concert down
below. I felt it only right and proper to stand by the rails watching the
lights of Dover as they slowly dipped into the horizon and think deep,
dark thoughts about mortality. I soon found this as unrewarding as the
night was cold, and went below.

Daylight, and we stepped ashore. Giving up all pretense, our half
dozen or so converged on Tony, experienced traveller as we assumed
he was, and almost literally clung to his coattail as he guided us to the
train for Paris. At this point the raison d'etre of the journey was tucked
well back in my thoughts for this foreign business was far more
enthralling. We all got into the same carriage, together with plenty of
natives, and what with looking at the passing scene, listening to the
incomprehensible chatter of our fellow passengers as well as envying

them their plentiful supply of food and drink with which they passed the time, the journey itself was more than enough to suppress odd thoughts about its end.

Not surprisingly, Paris itself was strange and bewildering, but we had no chance to stand and stare. Tony guided us to a large cafe in a grimy street. Someone answered his query with a nod of the head—upstairs. We obeyed and entered a room where many men sat eating and talking in half dozen languages. Charlotte Haldane, wife of J. B. S. Haldane, world-famous scientist and an outstanding "catch" of the British Communist Party, was in charge of this center for passing volunteers through to Spain.[9]

Very much a no-nonsense woman, she wasted no time on life's little courtesies but brusquely ordered various groups to sit, to eat, to finish eating and go, to wait for further instructions or, as in our case, to report. Then Tony, at our prompting, ventured to mention our slight and certainly unproven doubts about a man who had seemed to be trailing us and who was now sitting at a table on his own, eating. We took it for granted that Charlotte would respond in an appropriate corner of mouth and raised eyebrow manner. Instead, she silenced half the room at once with a sharp, loud command.

Show me! Point out the man you suspect!

We had no choice but to stop a few feet from the "suspect's" table and nod in his direction. By now everyone was watching and we would have been delighted to forget the whole thing. Gentle Charlotte was having none of that.

You! Who are you? Prove yourself!

The poor chap nearly choked on his food. Recovering himself he burst out in voluble French, obviously indignant, and he and Charlotte shouted and gesticulated at each other for a few minutes while the crowd of diners listened, intrigued, and we stood looking sheepish. Suddenly, with the other still in full flow of Gallic anger, Charlotte turned her back on him and walked away.

He's perfectly all right—a good French comrade.

We were given a table and some food. Soon, on Charlotte's instruction we left with an English-speaking Frenchman who was to take us to temporary lodgings.

We slept for two nights in a house in one of the poorer quarters of Paris. The minor discomforts were ignored in the novelty and strangeness of our surroundings. In the sparsely furnished bedrooms we exclaimed over the shuttered windows and the high, quilted beds; we were unsurprised that while *l'eau froid* gushed in the washbasin, *l'chaud* didn't. How many of us had "H&C" in our bedrooms at home? The loo, situated halfway up the several stories high tenement house and likely to be occupied by a squatting Frenchman or Frenchwoman indifferent to the absence of bolt or key, drove home the fact that we were now in France. These were precisely the kind of reports that made up almost the sum total of our knowledge of France or the French.

We ate in some cafe or other and were instructed to behave like tourists when we walked about the locality. Since few of us had much money, Paris had need of more well-heeled visitors to compensate for us. However, it did not take long for two or three more intrepid and less disciplined members of the party to discover the one remaining tourist attraction—a brothel! They told us how, by ignoring repeated instructions not to leave the immediate neighbourhood, they had gone into a more expensive cafe and were beguiled at the table by stark naked waitresses with obvious anticipations as to customers' requirements. Lack of cash brought disappointment to both sides. We others frowned severely at such unworthy behaviour, though we quite likely wished we had been there. George Baker and I, in compensation, walked to the nearby Pére Lachaise cemetery and saw there the reminders of another great struggle of the common people, the Paris Commune of 1870. On our way back we were accosted by girls standing in doorways, speaking words and making signs which needed no interpreter for full understanding. "No compro," we said, stoically if perhaps a touch wistfully. Next day our contact man gave Tony McClean instructions and money and we left at night for Lyon.

I liked the little I saw of Lyon, though in all these years I have never been back. We stayed for two nights only, in a quite pleasant hotel. Then we lost Tony. Nothing sinister in that, however, since it was the policy to split groups and use a number of different routes for the completion of our journey. The remainder of us departed, again at night, for Sete, a small town in the south coast. This settled our particular route;

we were to cross by boat. The alternative, used by the majority I believe, was to hike over the Pyrenees. I was not at all sorry to miss that—there aren't many mountains in Hackney.[10]

Our hotel in Sete was obviously inexpensive, but we were quite comfortable. Someone guided us to the Restaurant Espagne, where we were to eat free of charge. I remember virtually nothing of my introduction to foreign food but I am pretty sure I never turned my nose up at what we were given.

A local Communist Party member saw us each day and told us what news he had—or what he considered was enough for us. At first it was—"Tomorrow or the day after, you go." But when the day after that had passed he informed us that some delay was inevitable.

A brief note in my diary (not then in full stride) reads:

May 8th. Still here. Anarchist trouble in Barcelona delaying our departure.[11]

With no French-speaking member in our depleted party, this was all we knew. Just how serious the trouble was or, for that matter, what it was, we had no inkling. So we did not even begin to realise the implications and consequences for the Spanish Republic's life and death struggle which we were increasingly impatient to join.

"Be calm," said the local lad, "we will send you across as soon as possible. In the meantime . . . ."

In the meantime we were all getting pretty scruffy. The brightly patterned woolen stockings which went so well with my natty plus-fours now had large holes in heel and toe. We had been allowed, though reluctantly it seemed, one bath each at the hotel but blandly assuming the whole journey would take two, or at most three days, no one had brought even a change of underwear!

In Sete we gave up all pretense of behaving like tourists, which was just as well. The French, then as now, were strict in observance of their law requiring identification of every hotel resident. We were obviously considered to be at some risk and so had to be out of the hotel by 7 A.M. The cafe au lait at the Espagne was made to last as long as possible, after which stretched a weary time before we could return for the midday meal. Cash was very short indeed now. In fact, we were given a small amount of money each day, enough to buy a few coffees and a packet of Gauloise cigarettes. We went for long walks and spent much time around the lively and interesting harbor, and even more in cafes where we lingered as long as the natives over a coffee or beer. One morning we heard a radio tuned to London. It was Coronation Day, 12 May 1937. For my part it caused a short, sharp bout of homesickness, not for itself but because I thought of how 'the boys' would be out now, enjoying a ride in the Essex countryside, calling in here and there for a drink or a meal.

Another morning George and I were lounging over empty coffee cups. The proprietress came smiling to our table and spoke, in French of course. For politeness sake I smiled back and, for good measure, made a motion with my hand to head, eyes closed, which was the nearest I could get to bored.

"*A oui,*" she responded, smiling even more broadly, "*No probléme. Un moment.*" She went behind the counter, reached beneath it. Coming back to our table she gave each of us a small, foldover card.

"*No probléme,*" she repeated, pointing to the cards. We looked at them. On the front was an outline drawing of a partly draped female apparently admiring herself in a hand mirror. Madame was, we supposed, advertising the shop, name and address inside the card, which sold such articles.

"*Merci,*" we replied, politely, "*merci, Madame,*" and wondered why she should suppose we needed this particular service. At the Espagne we told the others of the incident. Tommy Chilvers, a very worldly-wise ex merchant seaman, burst out laughing. Turning the cards upside down he gave them back to us. We looked again and saw a very shapely young woman sitting naked in an extremely indelicate pose; the card was advertising a local brothel. Thinking about it I decided there was excuse for Madame's misunderstanding my sign language, and a basic logic in her suggested cure. She was not to know that we hadn't the price of even another coffee between us.

On Friday 14 May 1937, we left by boat for Spain—at night, of course. Strolling casually, as instructed, from our hotel we made our way to the harbour and were guided to an alarmingly small fishing boat. As our feet hit the deck we were at once whisked below to an evil-smelling hold. When our dozen or so were on board the hatch went down and there we were, in complete darkness and ordered to speak only in whispers.

At last, about 11 P.M., we sailed. And so began what for some of us was nineteen hours of misery and for all of us a journey into a new world. The sea was choppy, the boat small and built to carry fish, not people. The hold stank and was airless. But as soon as it was considered safe we were allowed on deck, a big improvement. The captain and his crew of two were Spanish. The captain's wife was also on board; we were told that he had in fact just come from fascist-occupied Majorca, having managed to take her away to the mainland. Several were ill for much of the time we were on board, but I was lucky, only occasionally feeling a bit squeamish. They gave us plenty of strong black coffee with hard, coarse bread and much harder dried fish. With daylight everyone felt better. We saw few other craft though once we were sent scuttling below when it was thought a warship of one of the Non-intervention nations was sighted. All such boats had the power, self-awarded, to stop, search, and arrest such as we. To general relief it was a false alarm. At length, land ahead! Spain was in sight and a green and pleasant land it looked to us; mountainous, too. Once again I was glad I had not hiked over them. At six in the evening we staggered ashore at Palamos, a small town on the northeast coast.

The hardship, the deprivations, the danger, would now be all too evident. We would not lack opportunity to prove our willingness to suffer with those whose cause we had taken as our own. Determined not to falter in our revolutionary zeal, we stepped from the boat half expecting to find a trench somewhere handy which we would at once man against all comers, fortified by dry bread and water.

Such ardor was a little premature. To say that we were escorted to the best hotel I had ever been in was not to say much, for until I left England Lyons Corner House had been a much more likely place of call than high-rating hotels. This one was very pleasant indeed. George and I shared a comfortable, well-appointed room with bathroom and loo en suite. Then we went down to a positively luxurious dining room for a satisfying meal. After dinner we strolled around the town, joining the parade, that almost obligatory occupation for the younger people at that time of evening. Needless to say, everything we saw enthralled and delighted us, not least the people, our Spanish comrades from now on. One slight hiccup, for which to our bitter regret we were not prepared: there was not a cigarette to be bought.

We went to bed early for our party was to leave by 4 o'clock in the morning. Inescapably, reality was taking the place of euphoria. The posters on boardings and walls, armed soldiers manning a checkpoint on the road out of town, a few cars painted in strange streaks of brown and green, made clear to us that we were in a country at war. Our honeymoon was over.

All so very long ago. Old men now, we had come back to this other Spain, over which Franco had ruled for nearly forty years. Since his death the people's new-found democracy still seemed precarious, uncertain. Only two months before our visit a Civil Guard colonel had held the Parliament at gun point. By a supreme irony, communists, socialists, Republicans, anarchists, and every freedom-loving Spaniard had been saved by King Carlos who repudiated the gun-toting colonel and all he stood for. But the would-be savior of Spain had spoken for a disturbingly large number of like-minded citizens. How would the people of Spain receive us, reminders of a nation divided in terrible and bloody strife?

We were soon answered. Next day, May Day, we joined the many thousands of Madrileños in a march through the city's main thoroughfares. Everywhere, marchers and onlookers greeted us warmly, embracing us, cheering our modest little banner which proclaimed us as veterans of the British Battalion of the International Brigade. The whole day was, for us, a triumphant progression. From the huge gathering in Independence Square to the feasting and jollifications in the Casa de Campo. Weary, and feeling our age, we reluctantly retired at midnight from the singing and dancing in the streets and squares, everywhere we had been received and feted as comrades and brothers. That night we slept soundly, hearts and minds at ease.

Saturday saw the start of our pilgrimage. We returned once more to the Jarama Valley and the scene of battle. Next to the battle for Madrid itself, this was one of the most crucial of the earlier struggles. In February 1937, Franco's troops began a well-prepared assault in the region with an immediate objective the cutting of the Madrid-Valencia road and, if all went well with his Moors, Germans, Italians, and even some Spanish troops, the ultimate encirclement of Madrid. Since November, when his Moors had so nearly smashed their way into the capital only to be repulsed by a rag-tag horde and a column of Internationals, Madrid had held out against repeated attacks. Jarama, Franco hoped, would end that.

It is not surprising that so much has been written about this battle. By then the International Brigades were a well organized, disciplined force, so not unnaturally they were called upon to play a major part in the at-times critical and always bloody fighting. The British Battalion lost many men here and had many captured—a number of whom were promptly shot by their captors. The valley became all too familiar to the British survivors. At the end of February the fighting died down, with the Valencia road and Madrid still denied to the fascists. For reasons no doubt quite valid to the High Command but only with difficulty appreciated by the weary troops, the British were required to stay in the trenches until the end of May. In fact, they had been gone only a few days when we novices of the Anti-tank Battery arrived in early June for our first taste of war. We had two weeks or so in these same trenches, then manned by Republicans.

Some old-timers from the February fighting were with us now. It was for all our first real getting to grips with our memories and emotions as we gazed around, trying to find tracks, sunken roads, buildings, which for so many years had been indelibly fixed in our minds. Yes, the valley is still there, and the river; we had just left the Valencia road, the ridge of low hills was easily recognized—but just where was that line of trenches? Or that small belt of trees under whose shade I had once, on guard by our gun, watched such a glorious dawn?

Sitting on a tree stump as the others milled around talking excitedly, laughing, pointing here and there, I slipped back into the past. And the past, with its memories and emotion, was so powerful as almost to become physical, alive: that time of being roused from the comfortable hotel bed at Palamos at 3 o'clock in the morning, given hunks of bread and a mug of black, sugarless coffee, then trudging still half asleep to the bus stop.

The bus was crowded, every passenger except us burdened with possessions, ungainly tied parcels, bulging bags, several dead fowl and, incredibly, one fortunately small live goat. Intrigued spectators, we sat in silence.

We climbed steadily higher and as the road twisted and turned we saw the dawn come up over the mountains, a stirring sight to us. At Gerona station we alighted and, after some hanging about, were put on a train for Barcelona.

Sunday, May 16th, 1937. Spanish trains lousy. Arrived Barcelona 9 A.M., very late. Taken to Barracks for meal. We leave tonight for Valencia on way to Albacete, Head Quarters of the International Brigades. Barcelona all barricades from recent P.O.U.M. fighting. Girls not so pretty as at Palamos! Strolled down the famous Ramblas and the

Plaza de Catuluna. Plenty of life everywhere, plenty of pretty girls, and soldiers—most in very smart uniforms. In my (now) extremely shabby-looking plus-fours I compared most unfavorably, but it did not seem important. Left, after seeing Grace Moore at cinema, at 11 P.M. Writing this on the train during one of its many stops.

"Barcelona all barricades." We had arrived within a few days of the savage in-fighting between the P.O.U.M. and the Government—George Orwell's finest hour. Much has been written about this tragic episode of the Civil War; all I feel qualified to say here is that as a direct result the Republican forces came nearer to a unified command.

Monday 17th May. Finally arrived at Valencia at 10 A.M. Train full of soldiers, several drunks. One kept taking pot shots at nothing through a carriage window with a revolver. No-one seemed to mind or try to stop him. Saw a little of the city till taken to get train for Albacete. In the Army now.

Left Valencia at 5 P.M., due in at Albacete at midnight. Finally arrived at 6 A.M.! Seems a much-bombed town. Taken to barracks of Assault Guards, fed, bathed *and given uniforms—woolen grey-green jacket, trousers rather baggy with elastic round ankles. Very happy to dump my old clothes, even though this is the winter uniform and we are well on the way to the hot weather here.*

No doubt our discarded civvies came in handy—even my plus-fours! But I certainly do not remember anyone being at all concerned about their safe keeping.

By now our party had increased to about thirty men. Some were gathered up on our journey at Barcelona or Valencia, having reached Spain by other routes, mostly over the Pyrenees, some were at Albacete awaiting our arrival. At Valencia we had been enrolled into the Army of the Republic of Spain. Now, in the bull ring at Albacete we became part of the International Brigade. Will Paynter, later General Secretary of the National Union of Miners, sat at a table and issued each of us with an identity card and paybook.[12] He then gave a short talk about what was expected of us, and how he was sure we would maintain the proud reputation of the Brigade. I still have the documents.

Later that day we were taken in trucks to the village of Madrigueras, twenty or so miles away. This was the training base for the British and

those of some other countries. Watched by seemingly incurious villagers
we walked along an unimpressive High Street to an equally unpretentious
one-time cinema or, more likely, theater. This was now our barracks. Loud
and somewhat ironic cheers greeted us from fifty or so men already in the
dreary, none-too-clean hall. These were mostly our predecessors by a
week or two, but also included some old hands. The latter understandably
considered themselves as elite and were very patronizing. For my part I
readily accepted them as the battle-hardened veterans they so willingly
allowed me to suppose. A few had indeed already been in action; some
had been wounded and were recently discharged from hospital. We listened eagerly to their stories. Later, we were able to make our own judge-
ments between talkers and doers. From many of the best and bravest we
heard hardly a single "I."

The only way I knew to come to terms with such living was to treat any
spot likely to be unchanged even for a day as home, and to settle for the
simplest comforts. This in fact was our home for the two and half weeks
of our training for war.

When we arrived the sun was hot, the skies for the most part cloudless.
Each day grew hotter yet and soon our military activities, never very
demanding, declined steadily. It was hardly a comfortable existence.
George and I took our straw pallets into a corner of the hall, used our jack-
ets for pillows and, like everyone else, made the best we could of it.
Washing facilities were poor but, oh, the loos! These were, in plain truth,
a disgrace to all concerned, including us. By the time we left they had
become so dreadful that few used them, preferring the fields. It was said
that prisoners would be sent to clean them up; even a "lifer" would
deserve a free pardon for his efforts.

The day began at 6 o'clock. We took turns to collect breakfast from the
central cookhouse in the village church. Coffee substitute (grim stuff, but
we were adjusting quickly!), bread and occasionally butter, this last a
well-meant gesture to our known tastes, even if of very poor quality.
Spaniards don't bother much about butter—not on bread anyway.
Sometimes a chap came round selling churros, a kind of rolled up piece
of fried batter, which made a change. Training started about 7 o'clock. As
I realized later, in the 1939-45 war, essentials seem to be much the same
in every army: forming-up, learning simple drills, and so forth. Frankly, I
can't remember that we took such activities over seriously, and discipline
was a tenuous thing, not to be tested unduly on unimportant frills. This
was especially true of some of the inescapable awkward squad who

badgered constantly to know when we were going to the Front—"To do
the job we've come here for, comrade, to fight the bloody fascists, not —
— around here like ponces." Discipline of a kind there was, but seemingly reserved for major offenses. I remember one particularly unpleasant
and aggressive character being marched off to the guardhouse, but he had
to clout our C.O. to qualify, while I would have been quite happy to see
half a dozen or so others keep him company.

Prior to Spain, most British volunteers were happy enough downing a
pint of beer. Wines, had they been affordable, were considered somewhat
sissyish. In Spain though, we took readily to the coarse red vino supplied
liberally at meal times and usually available in the cafes. To some the question of its potency remained a constant challenge, too often unresolved
until the questioner was beyond acknowledging defeat. Drunks were a
damned nuisance.

One day we marched to the armory and were loaned rifles, but no
ammunition. Under our instructors, Malcolm Dunbar, 2nd Lt. and Sergeant
John Black, with Hugh Slater as an amiable and decorative aide, we learnt
how to handle them, take them to pieces and even put them together
again without losing any bits.[13] Some rifles were old Lee-Enfields, others
from Mexico, some from Czechoslovakia; all were old or very old, the
sights were liable to differ one from the other, but at least they all used the
same ammunition. Two days later, when our turn came round, we collected them again together with five rounds of live ammunition per man
which we fired off in a local disused cemetery. We were also given, for
keeps, a tin hat each, the most uncomfortable, irritating headgear imagin-
able. I don't think many of us kept it for long. But all this helped to make
us feel like "real" soldiers as we marched off, rifles more or less at the correct slope on our shoulders, helmets on our heads and Miles Tomalin playing *Hold the Fort for We are Coming, Union Men be Strong,* on his
recorder.[14] Next day our military training reached its zenith when for a
few hours we played with and then fired two rounds apiece from a Maxim
machine-gun.

So the days drifted past and with each one hotter than its predeces-
sor we did less and less. It is easy now to say that so much more useful
preparation and training could have been arranged. From the beginning
to the end of the war the Government was under constant military
threat and, except in the overall determination to "Resist and Conquer,"
it was rarely able to achieve active agreement of all parties as to how
this was to be brought about. Among many practical difficulties was the

acute shortage of arms and ammunition. But perhaps the most important single factor lay in the International Brigades. We were the People's
Army, scorning the ways of imperialist armies. We were anti-fascists,
taking up arms to fight with the Spanish people against their destroyers.
Therefore, our place was at the Front, with rifle in hand. Our self-disci-
pline would show itself superior to the fear-inspired discipline of other
armies, certainly to that of Franco. This was no time to be playing at soldiers. Many of those who had marched in Madrid in November 1936
and helped to defeat Franco's advance on the capital, many who had
later held the Jarama and other Fronts, had gone straight into battle.
That many had died because of this was also true. But—"Any questions?" asked Sergeant Black at the end of a strictly nonpractical dis-
course on trench digging.

> Yeah, I've got a question, from one of our number.
> Good, said Black, encouraged by this show of interest, What is it?
> Pause, then—When do we go to the Front? Applause and "hear-hears."

With time on our hands we could at least carry out local expeditions.
Tony McClean, lost in Lyon, rejoined and was a welcome addition to our
small group. George Baker remained my steady pal, though we were often
with others. I remember Otto Estenson and his one-time shipmate, Tommy
Chilvers.

Madrigueras was a small pueblo, typical, as I later found, of so many
other villages or small towns in Spain; indeed it was this that made it of
such interest to me. Alone or with the friends I've mentioned I explored,
though haphazardly and with an untrained eye.

> *May 26th. All streets in this place lead to the village square, also the
> market-place. The roads and streets are shocking things of rubble and
> dust, with potholes a yard across or more—and nearly as deep. Mule
> carts have worn deep ruts in them, all of which makes marching a mat-
> ter of balancing on a narrow ledge!*
>
> *The houses are mostly one-storeyed, with narrow windows prison-like
> even to the bars, and shuttered, the shutters nearly always closed.*
>
> *The people are pleasant, friendly and courteous. The girls, up to about
> eighteen, are very pretty. But women show every sign of a hard life, and
> the old ones . . . . They dress cheerfully enough when young but soon go
> into black, complete with shawl. The girls too are friendly up to a point*

but, naturally enough perhaps, are more than a little chary of chance acquaintances. During the day they will stand and smile at us as we march past. At night the street in which we are barracked is choc-a-bloc with girls and soldiers. The unrestricted chatter of half a dozen languages is aided by two or three loudspeakers screeching out from cafés— news bulletins, popular songs, and always "The International," resulting in such a mixed grill of noise as I have never heard before. Occasionally a string of mules, homeward bound, adds its peculiar touch to the motley throng before disappearing through the front door of a house! But after 9oc or thereabouts suddenly the girls are gone, except for the lucky few with native male escorts. I have never seen any in the cafés.

I do not know how else these girls might work. But one thing they seem to be doing constantly during the day is getting water from the well in the square, which we are told is the only good drinking water in the village. They get it in pitchers and put the pitchers into handcarts which have holes cut in a board to receive them, usually four.

The Market Square is an important place. Market now is only once a week and only for odds and ends at that. One side of the square is a long cattle trough with the well usable at both ends. On the other side is the church, a rather big affair with a high tower.

As I later saw all too frequently, the church of almost every village in Spain was "a rather big affair," solid and strong. The dominant tower very often became a hated landmark, sheltering enemy machine-gunners. From Cardinal to parish priest, the Church kept its eye on the people.

There is no doubt the people here work hard. They are up very early and out in the fields. I have yet to see a cow in Spain, goats apparently taking their place as far as milk is concerned, and I prefer not to dwell on the subject of meat.

As for the ground—well, I admit that I know absolutely nothing about agriculture but to me it seems impossible that anything can grow in it. It is all like sun-baked, crumbly brickdust, stony as hell. Yet it is nearly all under some kind of cultivation. But even I could see that the implements used were almost primitive. Every night about 8oc herds of goats are brought in and an hour or so later we can buy glasses of warm goats' milk for 25 centimos.

Food is all rationed here. The people line up for different things. The cafés sell drink and little else besides.

For the first time in my life I drank champagne, a novel—and unexpected—treat for most of us. It cost eight pesetas a bottle, one day's pay. We noticed that the locals never bothered with it.

I wonder if the people here grudge us our regular, trouble-free feeding? I do not think so, and certainly if they knew the 100% lack of variety which, after the "coffee" and bread in the morning consists of stew four times a day—two meals of two courses each, exactly the same—they would if anything consider the regularity a punishment!

That stew was unbelievably bad. I am quite certain that not once did its composition alter. It was, unfailingly, a dreadful concoction of bits of meat (donkey? mule?), rice, and little scraps of potato all boiled together in olive oil into a most unappetizing mess. No one seemed to know what nationality the cooks were, though we were all quite clear they had been born out of wedlock and were now fascist. For all our revolutionary ardor I think we must have been a docile lot to have suffered as we did without protest. Except that it was not comradely to complain!

Once, and only once, a few of us were tipped off that there would be eggs at Matilda's café that evening for first comers. Skipping our stew, four of us went along at six o'clock sharp and were permitted to buy a meal of two eggs, fried, with bread and potatoes—in the preparation of which the olive oil had not been spared. We all paid heavily for such unwonted dissipation. On recovery we knew that for however long we were to be in Madrigueras, stew multiplied by four was to be our daily diet.

June 1st. Been here two weeks. Egotistically interested in my own reactions to this mass-living, which I have always disliked intensely. To my surprise find it comparatively O.K., but reject, rather too easily for my conscience, quite a number of "untouchables." Companies of Italians and Hungarians leaving to-day, raising another yell—"When?" from some of ours.

June 4th. Grand news! Leaving to-day. Also received two letters. In honesty cannot determine which is more important: to get the letters, very pleasant, or to search at once for the 8 or so Woodbines which are, or ought to be, inside. Squashed flat or not, these are definitely smokeable! All I can say is that to get a letter which does not contain fags is rather a let-down.

Later, same day. Blast, not leaving after all. Only 40 going and I'm not among them. Farewell party this evening for those going. Many drunks and two fights.

Saturday June 5th. And we are going! Grand news altogether. It appears that the thirty odd of us left including the officers and excluding the drunks and bloody nuisances (who are all in the first draft) are going for 10 days special training to form the first British Anti-tank Gun Battery.

We left Madrigueras about mid day. I've never been back. Sometimes, glancing through the notes I made at the time I'm sorely puzzled by my last entry from that village of which I have, on the whole, pleasant memories:

I'll always remember Madrigueras if only because of the sun, the glare, the dust, the flies—and the little children running along naked asking for money.

This last part bothers me, for I'm hanged if I can recall it. On the other hand, although my understanding of many events was no doubt often at fault, I'm positive I never invented.

We were taken to Albacete. At the barracks they had forgotten we were coming, or had never been told, and we had to sleep in the canteen— empty of goods. However, we willingly forgave them when we found hot showers available.

The next day, Sunday, we were on parade at 7 A.M. and, all very excited, were marched to the armoury, and there were the guns.

It was impossible not to feel a tingle of excitement as we looked at them. They were Russian, and quite new. Now they were ours. We crowded round and positively fondled them, our hands sliding along the polished steel of the long barrel, squinting down the rifled muzzle, kicking the big, heavy-tired wheels. Like schoolboys we took turns crouching behind the thick protective shield, pulling the breech open to insert an imaginary shell, a sharp upward pull to close it, then yelling "Fire!" as another pushed the red-painted firing mechanism. Removed carefully from its own wooden box, the telescopic lens was fixed in position and again we all lined up to look at the mystifying criss-crossing lines until we got the hang of it. We examined a few safe shells: there were two kinds, one had a pointed nose—that was the armor-piercing shell for use against tanks; the other had a small detonator which had to be inserted into the nose—that was the High Explosive, anti-personnel shell.

This was great fun. We were playing at soldiers in the pleasantest way possible, with no enemy to answer back. So we vied with each other in our martial posturing and felt very warlike. I think, if truth be told, there was a slight decline in this exuberance when Dunbar, our C.O., called us to order. For then we found just how big and heavy these guns were! Of course, trucks would transport them and us on journeys of any length (though we frequently found later that trucks were by no means always available) but basically they had to be manhandled. In the firing position the long and solid legs were splayed wide; on the order "Prepare to move," these were lifted by two men apiece, run together and clamped fast with an alarming clash of metal. Then with all eight of the gun crew placed at different positions, "Lift!," and the bods at the tail-end heaved up; "Move!" and as they pulled the rest pushed until, with much heaving and staggering and losing balance, the thing was moving. On a good, smooth, macadamed road it was relatively easy. Over rough fields with hillocks and deep ruts everywhere it was emphatically not. Hard enough when the "Heave," to get over some mound, lacked sufficient power so the damned thing (already?) rolled back causing the pushers to forsake all and scramble sideways with the barrel dipping to the ground and the two tailmen either jumping clear or being carried several feet in the air if they hung on. Worse still, though, when *one* wheel went down into a deep cleft in the ground, then the tail would be flung sharply to one side and woe betide any gunner who got caught by several hundredweight of solid steel!

Well, such fine points as these and many others were still to be discovered, often in circumstances unsuited to their proper appreciation. At that first introduction we were truly thrilled to think that we thirty-odd had been selected to man them—indeed, to own them, for from now on they were "our" guns. I was proud to belong to No. 1 Gun crew. George Baker was with me, as was Miles Tomalin. In command of all three guns was Lt. Malcolm Dunbar, with Sergeant Black as second in command. Hugh Slater was Political Commissar.[15]

It was an exciting week that followed, and even more interesting than any had been so far. Albacete was a fairly lively town. Despite, or perhaps because of some bombing, it had a purposeful air. People were busily going about their business and at all times the streets were thronged with soldiers of many nationalities, for Albacete was the headquarters of the International Brigades. Every day demonstrations and marches were a common sight. "Spanish Youth March Against Fascism!" "Workers, More Arms to the Front!" "Every Man to the Front!" ("What did YOU do in the Great War, Daddy?"). Shops were plentiful even with so little to sell. Cafés abounded and to our great delight there were some restaurants where we could—and did—have a simple meal of meat and potatoes. By then we were even getting used to the ubiquitous olive oil, though garlic, in the generous quantities Spanish cooking seemed to favour, was yet a hazard. At the International Club they twice had ice cream and beer, both, as I noted at the time, bearing a recognizable resemblance to the real (i.e., English) article. At all times there was an enthralling mixture of nationalities and tongues.

As we strove manfully to learn about the guns and how to lug them around with the minimum of exhaustion and bruises, we felt ourselves to be, at last, a part of Spain's fight; a small but, we were determined, an important part of this great working class force against fascism.

Of how that fight was progressing (no other, less optimistic word occurred to us) we learned little. Our Spanish, written or spoken was in its infancy. We tried our best with *El Socialista* or the communist *Mundo Obrero*; almost every day they seemed to be reporting Government advances here and there on the various Fronts or, at least, that our forces were holding their own. But one did not need to be astute to gather that something far from satisfactory was taking dreaded and ominous shape up in the Basque country. Bilbao, it was apparent, was doomed.

Significant developments were taking place on the political front, too, in May and June, following the anarchist troubles in Barcelona. Aware only of what we laboriously adduced from the newspapers or conversation, we readily accepted that these changes were for the best, and indeed we saw clearly that our cause had until now been hampered by yesterday's hero, Largo Caballero, as Prime Minister. Now, with Dr. Negrin (who *was* he?) in "No. 10," we could and would march forward to victory. At last Prieto, Minister of War, could plan the final triumph no longer held back, as Mundo Obrero snidely put it, by the timidity or worse of others.[16]

There was abysmal ignorance of Spain and Spanish affairs common to an overwhelming majority of volunteers from Britain. Recent events had thrust a country and its people to the forefront of our political consciousness. We rightly saw their struggle as an extension of our own in Britain. We went to help, to demonstrate the solidarity of working classes of other lands. But of the complexities of Spanish politics, the wide range of passionately held beliefs of so many parties from Liberals to Communists, not forgetting Anarchists and Trotskyists, Left Republicans and Separatists, we knew little or nothing. However, we had one invaluable yardstick to apply. Anticipating Churchill's famous declaration when Hitler invaded Russia— "Any enemy of Hitler is a friend of mine!" we said, with confidence, any opponent of Franco, of fascism, had us on his side.

At Albacete in early June 1937 we were, in our ignorance, pretty well satisfied with the state of the war and with ourselves.

Three days were spent in camp in beautiful surroundings near the village of Chinchilla. Here, with two other Batteries from different nationalities, we fired the guns, the unfamiliar, frightening noise shattering the peace of the valley. Anxious though all were to get cracking, the return to the stuffy, dreadfully overcrowded barracks at Albacete on Saturday night was a poor substitute for the delightful place we had just left. There was general pleasure in learning that we were to leave for the Front next day.

Sunday, June 13th. Up bright and early as usual. Definitely leaving some time to-day. Let out at midday for a meal which, as it promises to be our last in civilisation, some of us took at our own expense, accompanied by champagne.

It was not our last, though, for at 6oc we were taken to the Garde Nacional to eat and then brought straight back.

Everybody busy now. 15 guns, 30 gun-carriages (German and French Batteries are leaving as well).[17] Heaven knows how many boxes of ammunition and all our own gear to be loaded on train—open-sided trucks. All put on in complete darkness by 9 P.M. We are staying with the guns, on board.

We appear to be going to the Jarama Front, near Madrid.

Left at 10 P.M. Soon became bloody cold. Had been warned that the days became hotter and the nights colder towards Madrid. This one was certainly cold. But after one fire alarm (genuine, but not serious) went to sleep.

Monday, 14th June. Roused about 5am. Looked around for signs of war; saw usual peaceful landscape. Immediately had to unload guns and wait for transport by trucks. Told that rail junction for which we were bound near Madrid had been bombed. Issued with bread and bully for the day. It's bloody hot already.

4oc, and still waiting, all of us nearly dead with the heat. How people manage to fight *in it beats me. And to-night I suppose we'll be shivering again. Most of us, including me, are having tummy trouble.*

7.30 P.M.. At last cool enough to move around. Went down the road to the station and level-crossing of the Madrid road. Between two and three hundred people here, mostly women and children, milling helplessly about or sitting quietly on their bundles, waiting since early morning for a train to take them to Madrid. This place is called Temblaque. It would make an effective left-wing press picture: women crying, children squabbling, men helpless, armed soldiers holding up all cars, arguing, shouting and more shouting, bits of luggage everywhere.

Seems we are moving to-night. Right now waiting for transport from the 15th (English speaking) Brigade. The French leave to-night or tomorrow morning for their own Brigade, the 14th.

Tuesday, 15th. 6 A.M. Still here. French now loading their guns on trucks. Nothing to eat yet but promised some for 8oc.

Well well . . . Soup duly arrived by donkey cart from the village, but it was uneatable as far as I am concerned. Beans in olive oil. Not that it mattered much for with my stomach still troubling me it's best to lay off food.

Perched on top of a lorry just about to move off. It's about 2.45 now. All loaded on, including ourselves and guns hitched on behind. A train has just arrived and deposited masses more civilians, all of whom also want to get to Madrid. Some are trying to climb up on our trucks and we have no choice but to keep them off. Strange and depressing scene with hordes wandering up and down the road, crying and begging for lifts. Troops cleared the road and we left them there.

8.30 P.M. Easily the best and most beautiful ride I have ever had in spite of bumps. Splendid views. Circled round near Madrid. Went through Aranjuez, Parales, Tielmes, and eventually arrived at a place called Ambite, in a setting straight from the Sussex Downs. This is Brigade Headquarters. The whole 15th Brigade is about here, resting. We spend the night here. They gave us a good feed, and we needed it too. At last we are in the War!

June 16th. Got us up at 4.30 this morning. Now, at 7 A.M. we are in some olive groves about 1$^1/_2$ miles behind the Jarama Front. I believe that's how it's spelt but I'll check up later.

Very awesome to think that there is a real 'Front' just behind those hills.

12 noon. It seems that owing to the 15th Brigade having a well-earned rest from these same trenches, we are being attached to the 24th Brigade, a Spanish Brigade. Taken along to H.Q. and fed there then lectured by the 1st and 2nd in command. They impressed upon us how much they hope for from these guns, told us they are about 100 yards (!) from the fascist lines, and that they were sure we would uphold the tradition of the 15th Brigade which had been holding this sector. All this through a translator.

9 P.M. Now I'm sitting just behind the brow of a hill which is our front line. Below, on our side, is a beautiful valley surrounded by a range of hills. The Madrid-Valencia road is still intact and winds along beneath me. Some rifle and machine-gun fire disturb the otherwise peaceful scene. My feelings, naturally, are mixed. We are waiting for dark before taking our guns into the line. About 200 yards separate the trenches.

So here I am, essentially a man of peace, descending to the vulgar business of trying to kill. However, this time the end more than justifies the means.

June 17th. By 2 A.M. had our gun in position enough to camouflage it. Then slept in dugouts in the trench. Bloody weird to hear bullets whining overhead or hitting sandbags. Slept soundly all the same.

Woke about 6oc. Given coffee by Spaniards. Explored trenches. Most amazing labyrinth of lines, communicating trenches and dugouts. God knows how men stood four years of this in the Great War, in which they had no real interest. It is an incredibly stupid, filthy, primitive, barbaric business.

Fed quite well but water being short cannot wash. Sporadic firing continued all day. Engineers supposed to be coming up to-night to finish digging our gun in, and improve trenches around. So, to the usual accompaniment, ends my first day in the trenches.

Friday 18th June. Engineers did not come last night so gun remains in an exposed position. Fired five rounds at enemy machine-gun post. Reputed destroyed. Anyway, considering how quiet the Front is it must have given them quite a shock.

Engineers not arrived again, so we are going out ourselves.

Saturday 19th June. Out till 3.30 this morning digging in. Then after breakfast Dunbar came and told us we are to change our position to well over to the right. Oh well.

These bastard flies. Christ, there are millions of them. No spare water even for washing let alone shaving, so I'm getting an accumulation of beard and dirt worthy of any tramp.

9 P.M. Waiting for dark to begin moving the gun. I suppose the same old guys are doing the same old things at home. Must confess I would like an evening at the Robin Hood![18]

Sunday 20th June. Dawn rising over the fascist lines. Why is it that Saturday night always seems to bring some stranger event than usual? Last night we had just got the gun folded up and ready for moving when an attack started. In accordance with tradition it began on the stroke of midnight. For some strange reason we were ordered not to fire. Anyway, after about half an hour it petered out. We went on changing our position at 2 A.M. It takes all eight of us to shift the gun and exhausts the lot, ploughed fields, olive groves and trenches not making for easy progress.

So 5 A.M. found us having to hide the gun in a grove because the day came and we were not in position. In other words the gun is out of action for a day and we will be in action another night!

Now the others have gone back to our dugouts for some sleep. I, being on guard by the gun until 6 A.M., am writing this and watching the dawn, which is a good one, and thinking how blasé I have become regarding rifle fire and even trench mortars.

4 P.M. Now again I am on guard. Both sides seem to have Sunday afternoon feeling, and only an occasional shot disturbs the peaceful scene. Who, lying under the shade of trees, a beautiful, almost English sky above, would think that here the crux of this whole nasty business is being fought out?

Tuesday 22nd June. Got the gun dug in last night. No dugouts conveniently near here. We have just completed a shelter of sorts for ourselves, with no real hope that it will keep out anything more solid than rain and sun. Not quite so hot to-day though; in fact a few storm clouds about.

Wednesday 23rd June. What a night! And what a day so far. At about 10 P.M. a violent storm broke, and two minutes later so did our shelter. Just getting thoroughly miserable when all hell broke loose outside with, it seemed, every gun and rifle on both sides blazing away.

For two hours we slithered, fell and crawled about our gun, firing as rapidly as possible, aiming generally at the flashes from the fascist lines. Never did I imagine one could be so utterly uncomfortable. After two hours it died away (except the rain) and we went back to our useless shelter which, like the trench, had several inches of water in it. Our packs and gear were awash, nothing dry to put on, nothing warm to drink— just sit in our sopping bloody clothes waiting for day, or another outburst of firing. Daylight came but did not much improve things as it rained steadily until noon. What's it like in the real rainy season?

7 P.M. Gradually drying off, since the sun came out again about 2oc. Repaired shelter and now starting on real dugouts.

Thursday 24th June. At last, a good night's sleep, disturbed only by one and a half hour guard duty.

In the circumstances I think we eight get along pretty well. There is of course a fair amount of bickering, but this is inevitable living as we are. A chap named Croft is our sergeant, a decent enough fellow who knows how to handle the gun, and has been out here in Spain for about three months. But he hasn't the slightest idea of general leadership. He cannot pull the team together in a manner which is really essential if we are to live in any kind of communal serenity.

This life is one of strange and conflicting contrasts. Digging takes up a lot of our time and energy, but mostly we spend a lazing sort of rough— very rough—camping life. To-day the sun is shining and it is fine and warm again.

Fate was kind, perhaps, in allowing us such a relatively mild introduction to war. On this now quiet Front (expert opinion held that the flare-up on the night of the storm was nothing more than jitters on both sides) each of us adjusted in his own way toward an acceptance of the filth and discomfort, lack of sleep and hard toil. One and all, we closed our minds to what we knew was sure to come sooner or later, probably sooner. Unable to wash, except rarely, we dug dirt from our eyes, nose and mouth, accepted—albeit reluctantly—the myriad flies which swarmed everywhere, especially in the discarded trench we used as a latrine, and compared dugouts as, not so long ago, we might have contrasted the relative merits of different beds.

Quarrels were fairly frequent, though not overly serious. Oddly, in view of our self-appointed task, they seemed to reflect more chauvinist prejudices than personal animosities. When a minor fight started one

meal time in the narrow trench between a tough Scot and a rather
aggressive Irishman, English and Welsh combined to end it though not
before a foot clad in an extremely dirty boot had gone squash into a
dixie of potatoes. But I always found enough congenial souls to enable
me to make my own adjustment to this unreal existence and so, obviously, did the others. When it came to the crunch no one failed the test
of comradeship.

*Friday 25th June. The night until midnight was dark and threatening.
We all expected an attack, either from the heavens or the enemy. During
my guard spell several outbursts of rifle fire made me think something
was happening, but nothing came of it. Early this morning we fired off
nine rounds at what we think was a cookhouse.*

*Definite confirmation of the fall of Bilbao. This is bad. About a dozen
planes came over and dropped fascist leaflets!*

*Sunday 27th June. Some Brass Hats of the Spanish Brigade dug us out
last night about 11.30 and got us to send over ten rounds at the fascist
trenches. All done in a very casual manner and not a single reply from
them.*

*8 P.M. Apparently we have a busy night to-night. Got to take our gun
back to the previous position, over on our left, near our No. 2 gun. The
Spanish troops are making an attack with a view to taking some prisoners and we have to give them covering fire.*

*Monday 28th June. Midday. Oh hell. Got our gun where it was wanted
after two hours' bloody hard work. Very exposed position so we had to
dig like mad for three hours more to throw up some kind of parapet.
Attack timed for 4.30 A.M. Stood by until 5oc then attack called off.
Managed to get a few hours sleep this morning in old dugouts. Bitterly
cold last night. Now they say attack is for to-night—after which we take
our gun back again!*

*Tuesday 29th June. Another false alarm. Standing-to again from
11.30 until 4.30 this morning to support attack which didn't take place.
Apparently the moon was the trouble, too bright. Weather settled down
again to real heatwave.*

Wednesday 30th June. Quiet night, broken only by guard duty. Rumor has it we move soon for a "warmer" Front. Don't know.

Half dozed this afternoon in dugout and woke with a vivid impression of stretching out my legs in my own comfortable bed at home. Well, maybe again some day. How far away all that seems now.

After two weeks in the line I took my first shot at the fascist trench, at the invitation of a Spanish comrade who lent me his rifle for the purpose.

Taken all in all I don't for a moment regret being in the Anti-tank Battery. Being human I'm glad that we, I assume, will not be faced with the damned unpleasant task of personally coming to grips (probably with bayonets) with the enemy.

On Thursday 1 July, rumor became a certainty and we moved in the middle of the night. After a farewell concert with our Spanish friends in one of their biggest dugouts, during which we drank their vino and ate shreds of lettuce literally floating in olive oil, we were led by Miles Tomalin on his recorder in some suitable comradely songs, Spanish and English, and at last said goodbye to them.

Though we were glad to be about to join our own English-speaking Brigade, we were sorry to leave such fine chaps. They had helped us novices a great deal with their constant cheerfulness and friendship, their steadfast confidence in victory. The few treats which came to them from their families—though too many feared for the lives of parents, families and friends in Franco occupied parts—were ours to share. They were forever laughing when, that is, they were not swearing at fascism and Franco in the most vivid, filthiest imagery the effect of which was increased by the casual manner in which it was used. They went out of their way not to hurt our feelings, gently warning us that we were a long way from being the battle-hardened fighters we believed ourselves to be. In silence we got our gun out and moved off down the road, where the whole Battery assembled. We left the Jarama Valley behind us. Ahead, though undreamed of by us, lay one of the worst and bloodiest battles of the war so far—Brunete.

By the end of June 1937 the Government felt ready to launch its first really big offensive. The area chosen was around the small town of Brunete, twenty miles or so west of Madrid. The High Command hoped for a breakthrough that would relieve much of the pressure on the Capital. It was fought in the searing heat of the Castile plains for three weeks. In the battle the International Brigades played a very active part, with corresponding losses. We of the Anti-tank Battery quickly saw how right the young Spaniards in the trenches of Jarama had been when they laughingly assured us that our two weeks with them had been almost a holiday.

II

July-November, 1937
The Battle of Brunete

Saturday, 3rd July. Much to everybody's surprise the trucks arrived promptly at 4.30 this morning. Loaded up and left at once. Going straight in the direction of Madrid.

12 noon. Just my luck! Again dodged Madrid, rode all round the place through the outer suburbs. I should have liked to see it. Maybe there's plenty of time.

We are now pretty obviously bound for the Guadalajara Front in the mountains. Have stopped somewhere about 15 kilometres from Madrid, name unknown, here till dark. We have connected with our own British Battalion and the 15th Brigade. Terrific concentration of troops and guns etc all around.

Talk from Fred Copeman, Commander of the British Battalion, and from Bert Williams, he's the Political Commissar.[19] Copeman left us in no doubt as to the sort of time we are going to have here. It's the biggest thing of the war so far, and in his own words—"Sheer f.....g hell."

This evening we went down to the river which flows through a gorge between the hills and had our first all-in-wash for three weeks. Marvellous.

Sunday 4th July. Learnt something of our real position this morning. We are at Guadarama, not Guadalajara. Information: addressed by Malcolm Dunbar, our Battery Commander. He told us that about 100,000 men are engaged in this attack. "They" have decided to have a go at breaking right through the fascist lines in the direction of a place called, I think, Brunete, then working left in order either to cut off large sections of the enemy or else cause a hasty retreat for many miles along the Madrid Front. Told us the essential thing was to keep on attacking and that therefore we, by hook or by crook, had to keep up with the infantry. Since the advance is going to be over the mountains this won't

33

be easy. Trucks can only go so far up, the rest must be done by man-power. Water is practically non-existent there, wounded are brought down by mules. What food there is will be taken up by either mules or men. In other words, don't kid yourselves you're in for a good time!

Now, at dusk, the road up the mountain is crammed with troops, thousands and tens of thousands.

Monday 5th July. On the road by 10.30 last night. It took our truck about 4 ¹/₂ hours to travel 15 miles. Of course it was a very bad road, and it went up and up, round hairpin bend after hairpin bend. All the way it was choc-a-bloc with troops, trucks, mules, stores, guns big and small, and then more guns, more trucks, more men.

At about 4oc this morning reached a large, well-wooded ravine beside a stream. Camouflaged straight away. Told we stay here until to-night and then move up straight into the attack. Slept for a couple of hours, then had some grub. By dint of (accidentally, of course) sending two men from our team we got a double share of marmalade. This mar-malade has suddenly appeared in our rations and no doubt will as sud-denly disappear, but meanwhile, even without any marge, it's good.

Just lounging around now. This waiting for Zero hour is a funny business. Can honestly say I'm not nervous in the ordinary way but rather bloody curious, confident of victory, but not looking forward to lugging these guns about!

Tuesday, 6th July. Finally moved at 3.15 A.M. Then the long trek began again. This time many of our tanks helped the congestion.

7 A.M. On top of the world now, and the battle is there opening out before us. Down in the plain are villages held by the fascists and these our side have got to take. From just behind us our artillery is blowing hell out of the villages. This is big stuff, shaking the ground. Villages are on fire.

8 A.M.. Moved up another half mile. From here we have an almost bird's eye view. Immediately in front of our sector is a village. Dunbar says it's Villanueva de la Cañada, a mile or so away, which our troops are attacking. We Anti-tanks are apparently being kept for the inevitable check which will come—we hope after the village has been taken. We shall then move in.

About 25 of our tanks are closing in on the village. Our artillery has stopped. Troops can be seen behind the tanks. Village looks a mess through glasses (Dunbar let me have a look) but they are still fighting from positions in front of it. Horrible sight watching one of our tanks hit by a shell go up in flames. I hope the occupants were killed first.

9 A.M. Our artillery starting up again. Tanks holding back a bit. Can see smoke and hear firing from villages to right and left.

It is a very weird sight seeing the as yet unoccupied troops lining the brow of this hill, watching the battle.

12 noon. Village not yet taken apparently. Still fighting anyway. Another of our tanks has gone up in flames. Brigade H.Q. says we may have entered the village at one part. Difficult to see. We are still waiting for orders.

7.30 P.M. This is an amazing, incredible business. The attitude of the onlookers here is almost like that of spectators at Lords or the Oval. The groups of diehards, sitting through everything, maidens, stone-walling and all. Then those who prefer to go to the refreshment rooms and wait for an outburst of clapping to rush back for a good view, clasping their stone-gingers firmly as they run. So here, but minus the refreshment rooms, we wait for something more exciting than usual, then everybody rushes to the ridge for the latest developments. Only now, people are being killed and maimed down there—perhaps by now from the British Battalion, too. A few minutes ago six of our planes came over and bombed the village in front. This is now said to be ours in all but the final cleaning up, for which they are waiting for night. The villages on our right and left have been taken. We are all set to move off.

Wednesday, 7th July. Well, still here, though God knows why. The British Battalion is definitely in action. Village in front was finally captured about midnight last night. Our artillery and planes now bombarding villages farther ahead.

12 noon. Moved up now, through captured village (Villanueva de la Cañada) and about 3 kilometres along the road to small hamlet taken earlier this morning. And now, after three weeks without seeing a dead man, I've already had my fill. The road near the village was lined with about 40 of them, theirs and ours. Those who had been in the burntout tanks were not a pretty sight. The village itself was just a shell. Outside the village, more bodies as the fascists retreated. We've established ourselves under our old pal, "Olive Groves."

Enemy aircraft already active bombing the villages we have taken but not causing much damage since the troops have already moved on and the village was smashed up anyway. So far, of course, we have had jam on it—I mean our Battery. Can't see much here since we are down in a sort of plain.

6 P.M. Well, we've moved up now all right, bang in front of everything! All three guns of ours are up here, on a ridge with, below, a small stream and then another ridge—theirs! And not a man with a rifle between us and them. Getting dusk now and we have patrols out in front and behind, since that's where we are told our nearest troops are. Terrific bombing by enemy planes all round, and many fires. A number of British chaps, including some of our Madrigueras crowd, killed this morning.

Later that evening we met up with a few of the lads from the British Battalion who told us that in fact Villanueva de la Cañada had been very strongly fortified indeed with prepared trenches and strong points well placed. Dunbar confirmed that its protracted defense had been a serious setback to our attack which depended greatly upon a continued momentum for success. The British Battalion had taken part in the final assault and suffered severely. A horrible tale they told us perhaps had something to do with the bodies of women we had seen by the roadside. Moving into the final approach they had seen some women coming along the road toward them waving their arms and shouting. Confused, our troops stopped firing; then from behind the women and using them as a human shield, came the fascists, taking heavy toll of the attackers caught off guard. Unavoidably, many women, it was said, were killed, too. This tale has become part of the legend of Brunete. I have not spoken to anyone who actually saw it happen.

Thursday 8th July. A company of Franco-Belge came up from behind us during the night. They kicked up a hell of a row as though they were at a football match, fired off rifles, lit lights, pinched some of our stuff and then sheered off. Lot of fighting over to our right but unbelievably we spent a quiet night what was left of it!

A Spanish Battalion came up from our rear this morning and advanced, going over the river and attacking the ridge on the other side. What the hell we do about it, God knows; we've had no orders of any kind yet. Getting very dirty, and fed up with bread and jam. Once again we have a bird's-eye view of the fighting but need glasses. Either we are the world's luckiest bastards or else we are going to pay for this pretty soon.

2.15 P.M. And from 5 minutes after . . . .

Friday 9th July. Jesus! What a couple of days. My God, but I'm tired, tired, tired, hungry as hell, thirsty and filthy. At about 9 A.M. yesterday as we were preparing to fire, on orders from Brigade, enemy artillery got our range. We hoped it was just luck, but they got bang on to No. 2 gun with their third shot, killing two. We got to hell out of it with the guns. Only to just behind the ridge, but after a few more shots they stopped, so obviously they had us sighted all the time. No wonder, seeing the bloody silly way we wandered about there in full view.

At about 11 A.M. we were ordered to move over to the other flank. Trucks arrived down below the hill, we hitched up and were off. Then suddenly enemy bombers sighted us before we sighted them, and bits of the road and fields nearby went up in the air. Trucks stopped and we scattered. This happened twice and each time too near for my liking, though no casualties.

Eventually we crossed the river and then were kept at the roadside several hours awaiting orders, and under bombardment from their planes almost the whole time. It's just the world's worst bloody sensation—flattening out with your face in the dirt, shrapnel and muck falling all around and on top of you.

About 8 P.M. it finished; only one of ours wounded, very lucky.

Saturday 10th July. And now, thank God, yesterday has gone and, even more important, most of to-day. And much to my surprise I'm still alive. This concentrated, accurate shelling from their big guns is sheer hell.

Maybe when this battle is finished and if I'm still alive I'll fill in some more details. Two more of ours killed, and one wounded. Goodness knows how many infantry.

Sunday 11th July. Another bastard day. Went back to our old post up the road last night—we'd had to get out in a hurry the day before, and had to do the same again to-day; they shelled us heavily with more big stuff. Lucky to get down into the valley for an hour or so. Two killed, including Black, 2nd in Command. One fellow, from Battery H.Q., skipped it. Numbers very reduced.

Brigade H.Q. say satisfactory on each part of different fronts except our sector where enemy tanks are mucking things up for us. General news good. France, Russia and Britain (!) reported to be withdrawing from Non-intervention!

One lovely hour's quiet.

Monday 12th July. Another night minus sleep. Four running—our crew are practically all in.

Had to get the gun back to behind Base, which was blown almost to pieces yesterday. All six of us (!) digging dugout a few yards back from the gun. Too damned tired to make much headway.

And never will I forget the cheerful sod who chose to pause in his labours to say-

We're just digging our own graves . . . .

He nearly started a private war, only the rest of us were too exhausted to do more than swear at him.

Haven't washed for a week—water non-existent. Food, bread and jam at infrequent intervals.

Wednesday 14th July. The tumult and the shouting dies—for a little while anyway. Both sides are now licking their wounds. The Government has advanced about 8 miles, which is a lot of ground, but our sector seems immovable now, and friend and enemy are digging like mad.

Out of forty at the start we have lost fourteen, which means each gun is being manned by six men.

It's a pity we haven't more aeroplanes. Theirs seem to come over when and where they like. Half a dozen times a day at least we are being bombed.

Last night we were out doing odd jobs until 1oc. The sky was amazing. Ominous storm clouds had arisen (we remembered Jarama!) and the sky was a deep black. Then their planes came over and dropped dozens of incendiaries. The usual fires were burning here and there, and searchlights looked for the planes. Add to this very effective, and very beautiful, lightning, and the picture presented by earth and sky was, in the fullest sense of the word, awesome. Anyway, no rain fell, there were no attacks, we had a couple of hours sleep.

In the early morning we had completed a really good dugout which would hold the six of us when we were not actually by the gun. And at 8 A.M. received orders to get the gun out ready for moving. That's what it's been like all the damned time. Dig, dig, dig, gun in, some kind of shelter ready; then—gun out, get ready to move. Still, can't be helped.

Anyway, we are going into reserve for a couple of days to enable the Brigade to re-organise prior to another go at the ridge which is holding us up.

This was the infamous, so-called Mosquito Ridge to which so many accounts of this battle refer. Most competent authorities agree that had this been taken at the first assault the whole outcome of the battle might well have been very different. As it was, the Ridge claimed many, many lives, and remained in fascist hands.

The water wagon stopped nearby us; for the first time in 10 days I washed!

Thursday 15th July. Well, here we are right behind that cursed house from which we were shelled four days ago. Our big guns have moved up and are now banging away just back of us, so we are not getting much peace. Still it's good to know that we haven't got to rush to our guns any minute—though we have had to put them in reserve positions, just in case.

Friday 16th July. The comparative peace of this spot was rudely shattered this morning by combined bombing and shelling, both coming much too close. This sort of thing is utterly demoralising if kept up long enough. And our food always suffers by it, for the cookhouse is about 15 miles back and food is brought up by truck. God knows, anything approaching real food is rare and irregular enough at best, but when an air-raid or bombardment is on, well . . . .

I'm afraid I am not yet sufficiently calmed down from the effects of the last week to write anything as to what I feel about it all. I will merely say that Jarama would indeed now seem like a holiday.

Non-intervention has finished, apparently, and everybody now expecting great things.

We hear that 600 fascists have shot their officers and come over to us; 2000 prisoners taken during this advance, 25 enemy planes shot down during the last couple of days. Certain it is that, looked at from an impersonal point of view, things have gone splendidly, in spite of that bloody ridge which is definitely holding us up now. But, as Dunbar says, something of the kind was inevitable.

Saturday 17th July. At the moment of writing (midday) we are having another test of endurance from their artillery. They are probably looking for our big guns, just behind us, and are using us as a sort of starting off point. I wish they would not. Still no orders for moving up again. We think they are waiting for more troops.

*Sunday 18th July. The fateful 18th July. One year ago to-day this busi-
ness started. And as might be expected there is quite a lot of activity this
morning. In the early hours there was a terrific artillery duel. Then came
a formidable air-raid of about 30 planes which did their stuff a little too
near for our comfort. In the middle of all this someone started an attack
over to our right.*

*Suddenly swarms of "grave-diggers" (an unfunny name used by most
of us when referring to troops roughly corresponding to our own British
Pioneer Corp) descended upon us from the direction of the attack, and
obviously running back. This was disturbing but not much information
could be gathered from them except that the 15th Brigade was retreating.
We made no sense of that, for the 15th, like us, are in reserve. However, a
runner came from Brigade H.Q. with the news that nothing had happened apart from the fact that for some inexplicable reason a few of these
"grave-diggers" (who, after all, were armed with only picks and shovels)
had been seen to run and others had followed suit. But it also appeared
true that the fascists had in fact tried a two-dimensional attack and some
of the famous "Listers" had retreated a short way, hence the scramble.[20]
Anyway, the attack wasn't much, but two battalions of our 15th are digging in just in case.*

*This incident was strangely like that of Sunday last when we were in
that ghastly position up on the road and at about dawn a couple of hundred Spanish infantry came suddenly flying back like mad to the road
right alongside our gun, crying that the whole line was retreating and
the fascists were at their heels.*

*As it happened that was a false alarm, but about 3oc in the afternoon
we received orders to fire on the opposite ridge and no sooner did we
open up than they showed us they had our mark perfectly, for over came
their shells bang on to us. Getting that gun out, between shells, across the
road, which they were machine-gunning, and down into the valley was
one of the worst experiences of my life.*

*That was a week ago. And all the other details of this battle which I
have left out in the stress of the moment—such as the blowing up almost
in its entirety of our Base and Battery H.Q. and our ammunition, the terrific fight which took place on the day Black was killed, the sheer hell of
sitting in the blazing sun hour by hour waiting for an attack—all these
things, too, are over, and we must get used to them for come again they
will, very soon, I think.*

Had a letter to-day. Quite a few I must answer, but don't seem to have the energy.

6 P.M. A little bit of variety provided by a real prairie fire caused by incendiary bombs which, aided by a strong breeze, came rushing up almost within reach of our guns and trucks. After an hour's hectic work succeeded in stopping it. Then, as a change from common-or-garden bombing, we had a first-class aerial battle right overhead. There seemed not to be any casualties. Now their artillery is having another go.

I shall be glad when the 18th of July is over. In any case it strikes me that, short of an all-out battle, it is a damned sight quieter in the line! By the way, it's rumoured we go in again to-night.

Tuesday 20th July. Just scribbling this lying in a dried up river bed, sheltering from artillery. We've moved, over to the left flank and are in position. Not much idea where we are, but can see that damned ridge again. In fact, quite clearly, though from a different angle.

Later. Fired many rounds at various targets on or about the ridge.

Wednesday 21st July. Have dug ourselves in a little right by the gun. Food shortage is causing some discontent among the crews. Until an hour ago we were shelling enemy machine-gunposts. I think we move again soon. Waiting for reinforcements before the attack on the ridge starts up again.

Later that afternoon fascist planes came over once again and this time I was hit. Badly enough from my point of view, but not critically. I had shrapnel in the calves of both legs and—to complete the symmetry—a fortunately small piece neatly centered in my backside! So ended for me the Battle of Brunete.

The battle continued for another six days or so of increasingly severe counter attacks by the fascists until much, though not all, of the hard-won gains were retaken. I cannot argue with the later verdicts of experts who declare it was a defeat for the Government in terms of the horrifying losses of men and material in relation to those of Franco. I simply state my conviction that to the troops it was a great morale booster, proving that we could stage a major assault.

News of the ending of Non-intervention proved utterly untrue, of course, and I never heard any more of the so-called revolt on their side.

It took a long, long time to get me away from the field after I had been hit. George Baker, already my buddy, was right by my side when it happened and he with others dragged me back down the ridge a little to a hollow which was being used as Battery H.Q. and was relatively safe, at least from shelling. There I stayed for some hours, with a first-aid dressing on each leg and a large pad at my rear. I remember great discomfort rather than pain at first, an unpleasant feeling of stickiness. I am sure I was not so reasonable at the time about the delay. It was, I know, no more than the other side of the coin of our being a small, separate unit. In many ways this was an advantage to us, but we felt the lack of all the auxiliaries which were attached to the Battalions. So messages had to be got to Brigade Field Hospital, who were no doubt extremely busy. But eventually they came along with a stretcher and carried me to the nearest usable road. From there an ambulance took me and others to what was, I suppose, Brigade Clearing Station. Again I spent a considerable time lying on my stretcher on the ground, and it was then that an element of farce crept in. It was quite dark by now and a very strange scene indeed. There was a great deal of running hither and thither, much shouting, more wounded arriving on stretchers and by ambulance, torches flickering on and off, cries of distress and pain from some. I could see others like myself waiting to be taken away. Some medical orderly had replaced my field dressings with more care and skill but he and everybody else spoke only Spanish, so there wasn't much communication going. With a not very clear idea of just how badly wounded I was, the increasing pain, stiffness, and general discomfort did nothing to reassure me. Added to all this—I wanted to pee! In fact, this need rapidly became most urgent, but no one whose attention I did manage to secure could understand my puzzling distress calls. Even then, in that time of dire necessity, I was incapable of throwing off those "Good manners" lessons learnt at my mother's knee: had I been able simply to undo my fly-buttons and point . . . . Finally, and just about in time, someone came along who spoke English!

I had another worry, too. The safety of my diaries. Although at that time I was only on Book Two and, as always, kept them on me, two or three stray helpers about this place had made passing attempts to take my clothes in exchange for a blanket. Each desisted, I am sure, rather for being called to more pressing matters than because of my endeavors to explain to them that I wanted to retain a notebook from the back pocket of my carved-up trousers and another from the inside pocket of my tunic and would they please take them out for me.

Hours later that problem was resolved by a friendly nurse when, finally, an ambulance deposited a load of us in hospital in Madrid. It was what had been, and is now again, the Palace Hotel, 5-star and all the trimmings. At last I was staying in a posh hotel! Let me say at once lest I forget later, all the doctors and nurses I met there were Spanish, and I could not have wished for kinder or more compassionate people.

Lying safe in hospital, I delighted in the luxury of a comfortable bed, clean sheets, a cool shady room, peace and quiet. There was, too, overwhelming relief that the constant stark fear of the preceding three weeks had ended. As the days and weeks passed I faced up to the bleak reality that sooner or later I must be prepared for more of the same. Gradually the emotionally charged atmosphere of the time and place helped blur the sharpest edges of the worst horrors. But some defied all my homespun therapy, until augmented and even outdone by later battles.

Many times I relived the day Black was killed. How it came about that George Baker and I were in a trench which seemed to be the focal point for all the fascist fury I don't recall. Jock Cunningham, of the 15th Brigade Staff was there, issuing orders, sending messengers right and left, endeavouring to cope with what was obviously a critical situation.[21] Then, as the telephone operator at his side failed repeatedly to contact some required unit, Cunningham saw us.

Your two, get this f——g message to them quick, and there's only one f——g way, over the top!

Even now the memory is still vivid. A fierce fascist attack was raging and, as George and I edged ourselves cautiously over the parapet of sandbags, bullets whistled and cracked past us. For perhaps fifteen minutes we crawled about, never daring to lift our heads an inch from the dirt, shrinking into petrified hulks when a shell or mortar burst nearby. Then we gave up. I clearly remember that getting back was even worse; it is much more frightening when it's all coming from behind you! Falling ignominiously into the trench we confessed our failure to deliver the message.

What message? asked Jock.

One of so many incidents. I found, though, that swapping tales with fellow patients helped. Too often in their personal accounts there was no fear, only great courage, and I realised that they too were anxious to come to terms with human frailty. It was only that their remedy was different from mine.

I was soon able to resume my scribbling.

Saturday 24th July. It's grand to hear city noises again. The peace and quiet inside here is beautiful. But it is tragic to hear, from time to time, the boom of guns from the Casa de Campo and the crash of shells falling into poor old Madrid. They are not really near us, but always afterwards we hear the clanging of bells from ambulances and fire-engines.

Sunday 25th. Very few English here, and nothing to read. But yesterday a chap came round with some English books. I bought three for 20 pesetas.

They have just told me that I change hospitals either to-day or tomorrow. Hope it's tomorrow for one of the Spanish attendants made it plain he would buy me some toothpaste and a brush, for which I gave him 15 pesetas. Money is now short. I came in here with 50 and now I could do with drawing some of that back pay owing me.

Tuesday 27th. Took us out about 4.30 yesterday afternoon. Met up with Otto Estenson. He had a bullet through his right arm. We travelled together, he sitting in a motherly fashion by the side of my stretcher. He is one of our Battery, a very fine chap. He tells me there was something of a retreat during the last two days and that the fascists had got back Brunete.

Eventually Otto and I, with a dozen or so others of mixed nationalities arrived at Huete, a small town in the province of Cuenca. We were taken to a huge building, a one-time monastery now used as a hospital. And there I stayed until November!

The hospital was administered by British personnel though from time to time Canadian and Americans also served there. Renee and Isobel came all the way from New Zealand to add their skilled competence to the nursing staff. Way down in the pecking order came the Spanish doctors, nurses, and many orderlies and general workers, all of whom made possible the well-thought of English hospital. For most of my protracted stay Doctor Tudor Hart was in charge.[22]

He was a remarkable man. (He had, too, a remarkable sense of humor. Once, having just amputated a man's leg he remarked quite jovially—"I could play with that for hours.!") A very friendly chap when all went as he planned, he could be quite brutally rude and overbearing if put out. Of his and his fellow medicos' skill I am not really competent to judge except that I was, so to speak, on the receiving end.

That my stay was so long was due, largely, to one or other of the frequently changing staff finding yet another fragment of steel in one or both legs. They seemed to regard this as an impertinence, a slight on their expertise, that such an object should have evaded their most recent probing: x-rays were used sparingly then.

Very late in this game a dear, elderly, plump Spanish nurse, delightfully named Candida, who claimed residence for some years in Bristol and whose English was infinitely superior to my Spanish, suggested with due humility that the latest find might safely be left where it was. Hart was horrified. Down to the operating theater I went yet again.

I soon made friends with many of the hard working staff, British and Spanish. On the other hand, and somewhat in the nature of a confession, quite a number of the patients occasionally brought out the worst in me. I've never been a truly gregarious bloke, and in hospital was often driven to distraction by noise and general foolery and, especially, by the endless repetition from the few compatriots there of the minutely detailed accounts of how they came by their wounds. This was particularly trying during lengthy spells confined to my bed, a helpless victim. Every new batch of wounded brought yet more of these tormentors. When, at long last, these were at least temporarily silent, Sam was still there.

5th October. I must make a note of Sam Parkes, in case I forget the unforgettable!

I need not have bothered. Poor Sam was truly unforgettable. He was one of many who should never have been allowed to go to Spain. A very amiable fellow, he was also very dim. In the hospital or out in the town he slopped around in pyjamas and rope-soled slippers. One arm and shoulder were swathed in bandages, the arm itself cradled out at right angle in a cast. The bullet hole in his shoulder would eventually heal, but the arm would never regain more than fractional use. To hear him make light of this caused embarrassment to his listeners rather than admiration for his courage. Wearing a fixed grin almost permanently he made it clear he just did not understand that he had been hit for six; that in a world where, for one thing, work was scarce, he would never be at the front of the queue. In a mixed up, cockeyed way he enjoyed his self-created role of The Man Who Had Been Wounded in Spain.

He went about the wards of the hospital telling all who would listen—

"I came to Spain for adventure and . . ." He could not trust his listeners to get the point unaided—"See this? Well, I got it!" And a broad grin would spread over his face as he peered intently at his victim. Assured of complete understanding he would roar with laughter, in real genuine appreciation of a fine joke.

We never saw anyone who had known him in his unit, he did not receive letters from home. He told us he had been out of work a long time before volunteering for Spain, that he had no idea what it was about, but—and then the depressing repetition of his tale.

Sam was the butt for many jokes and pranks. His desire to be friendly with all made it difficult to defend him from some of the nastier elements. He had been in hospital a long time but the Army had not yet got around to paying his (or anyone else's) arrears of pay. So he was always broke and quite prepared to scrounge. His smattering of Communist Party jargon would be tried out with servile manner and bearing so dreadful to see, worse still to receive directly, that it made one desperate to avoid. Thus, to a man unwisely counting his pesetas openly:

> To each according to his needs, eh comrade? I bet you're another one who
> came to Spain for adventure, eh? You got it, too, didn't you? Like me, ah? You
> got enough for a drink in the village, comrade?

The Spanish nurses were generally kind to him, though the younger and prettier found little to recommend him; he was no Errol Flynn. He remained as unaware of the compassionate looks and little extra treats he had from thirty-five year old Anita as he was of the intense dislike darting from the black eyes of seventeen-year-old Pilar, immaculate every day in her fresh uniform dress, shining with cleanliness and youth. Combing his own none-too-clean hair one morning with a positively dirty comb, Sam reached out his good arm and, as one might with the certainty of doing no wrong, caress a baby's face, ran his comb through the girl's lovely hair.

His Spanish was almost nonexistent, so it was her gestures, her eyes, her obvious loathing at what he had done more than the words she spat at him which persuaded him that life had unexpectedly and inexplicably smacked him down again.

Sam did not like the food, of course. Like a great number of us he had eaten too many fish and chip dinners varied by sausage and mash, or pie with mash and lots of parsley gravy, to take kindly to garlic, or a few leaves of lettuce and a small piece of cheese swimming in a dish of olive oil. It was rare, in fact, to meet anyone from Britain's "lower classes" who actually enjoyed Spanish food. Sam reckoned he "Just can't get on with it. Funny ain't it? They just don't have the same kind of grub as us. Funny ain't it?"

A new hospital Political Commissar quite fell for Sam at first. He made his introductory visit one morning just as the English nurse in charge was doing her rounds. Sam, with his impressive array of bandages over shoulder and chest, his right arm giving a permanent clenched-fist salute, appeared a certain "right response" man to the Commissar.

Salud, Comrade, said he. Where were you wounded?

Sam's grin widened and his mouth opened to tell this chap that he had got it in the bloody arm after coming to Span for—but the nurse popped a thermometer in and saved his story for another day. Of course, it was not long delayed, and Wally learnt to dodge him with the same readiness as, I am afraid, did the rest of us.

For months I wondered what became of Sam. Complete recovery in Spain seemed unlikely; common humanity demanded he be sent home. If not, then perhaps his very simplicity might have persuaded Franco and his fascists to take him on as an outward and visible sign of their Christian charity. They were very good at that.

In fact, long afterwards, I did meet Sam again, still in Spain, still in hospital.

Meanwhile, in Huete, the days and weeks passed slowly.

Saturday, 7th August. Life is now one long round of waiting for meal times. Thank God there is a fair number of books here. I have just finished a good one, By-road, *by Adrian Bell.*

I wonder how the War is going. It's damned difficult to get news. In the meantime the 15th Brigade, including the Anti-tanks, are at rest in Mondejar, which is the place where we first came upon them, near Ambite.

12th August. I'm 26 to-day! For, I think, the second time in my life I
had a birthday cake—only I bought this one myself. Twenty five pesetas,
quite cheap, and not too bad, just enough for all the ward to have a
small piece each, including my chief tormentor, the guitarist.

Three or four days previously an influx of really serious cases had
caused the removal of some of us to another ward where most were
mobile, noisy, and unruly. With few restrictions from authority they
kept a concert-like atmosphere going for most of their waking hours.
One young Spaniard, proud owner of a guitar, strummed away tire-
lessly. His favorite was "Three o'clock in the Morning," which he played
over and over.

However, after more, and painful, probing in one leg or the other, I
returned on the 14th of August to the comparative peace of Ward D.
Each ward had one man elected by the others to be responsible for
orderly behavior. In theory it was a good idea. But in such a mixture of
nationalities, types, temperaments and, most important perhaps, the
almost total absence of more forceful if less comradely discipline, it fell
short of its desired end. Never an easy mixer myself I nevertheless had
positive views on the line dividing social and anti-social behaviour. So
there were, I'm afraid, many times when I found my comrades-in-arms
singularly lacking in life's little courtesies and even occasionally elemen-
tary (to me) decencies.

Access to the town was simply a matter of having two legs, or even
one, to get you there. Wine was cheap, some of us had money, so from
time to time the ward was enlivened by two or three drunks returning
noisy and garrulous. Once, a group of Frenchmen was admitted, none so
seriously wounded as to prevent their immediate departure for the town.
That night saw just about the lowest level in international relations of the
whole war! To the relief of all, Spaniards, British, Americans, and Italians,
the Frenchmen were so outraged by the absence of anything stronger than
synthetic coffee at meal times that they demanded, and readily obtained,
transfer to another hospital.

One Frenchman, though, lay quiet and indifferent to his compatriots'
clamor. Francois, twenty years old, had been in his corner bed in the
ward since February. With a bullet lodged in his spine he was paralyzed
from the waist down and was slowly dying. Too ill even to speak much,
he was dependent for every need upon that most compassionate of
nurses, Anita. The daily washing and bed changing was, for the whole

ward, a very noisome hour. Anita went about it as to a pleasant task, smiling and making little jokes to him as she worked. One day, her usual helper absent, she called to the beautiful Pilar. Reluctantly approaching the bed the young girl put her fingers to her nose and made a gesture of disgust. I did not hear what Anita said to the girl, but it was enough to silence her for the next couple of hours and bring a blush to her face.

Poor Francois spoke virtually no Spanish; few spoke French, certainly not Anita nor I. How it came about that I knew the French for cheese I can't imagine. But once when Anita was trying so hard to see if there was not some little tid-bit to tempt the poor fellow, I heard him gasping out one word over and over to the puzzled and distressed nurse. Then I caught it—fromage—.

"Cheese," I called out from my bed, then, remembering, "Queso!" It was hard to see which was more pleased, Francois or Anita, as she returned in triumph with the small piece of cheese she had begged from the kitchen for him.

Months later, when I was again in hospital, though not Huete, I learned that Francois was dead.

Anticipating letters and fags became the major concern of most days. The main recorded event of 3 September was the receipt of seven letters, from which I accrued 25 Woodbines.

I continued up and down from the operating theater and back to the ward almost like a yo-yo. I know now that even in those days medical expertise was such that, given the necessary drugs and equipment—and there's the rub—my wounds should have been healed in half the time.

On 3 October I was allowed out into the extensive gardens. Then I was back in bed again for a week! I did not mind so much this time, for the weather was changing. Too often now it was cold and wet. There being simply no question of heating this vast, cavernous place, it was warmest in bed.

Some days brought their hilarious bursts of excitement, relished in different ways by every one of us. In the middle of October a report swept through the hospital that two priests had been caught hiding in the town. This had the more dedicated anti-clerics among us straining at the leash to show their mettle. Men more mobile than I told me the two were now temporarily lodged in the local gaol, reportedly situated in some part of this one-time monastery. Late that same evening, more excitement: a fire, in that part of the hospital adjoining the prison.

Sabotage! Fascist prisoners had started it, planning a mass escape. Of that there could be no reasonable doubt. Our righteous anger knew no bounds. "Give me a rifle," demanded Ed Bowers, one of several American patients, "and I will shoot the bloody lot!" We learned later that a kitchen chimney had caught fire but was soon put out. Nothing more was heard of the alleged capture of the priests.

Frustrated in his wish to shoot a few, or many, priests, Bowers left a much more pleasing reminder of his stay in Huete. Walking patients ate in a long, narrow vaulted room below ground level. Ed used one end-wall quadrant to paint a very fine mural. Unfortunately, my photo of the finished effort is lost, but I remember how cleverly and pleasingly he brought life to the popular slogan: "Fight and Work to defeat Fascism!" Ed was, I believe, killed some months later. His memorial would not have lasted much longer.

Visitors of note occasionally came to see us. Arthur Horner, South Wales Miners' leader, gave me cigarettes and a copy of *Cwmardy*, a story of the Rhondda by Lewis Jones.[23] One or two of my Battery comrades called in on their way to or from other places. They had not neglected me entirely, for I had received letters from several, especially George Baker and Miles Tomalin.

Gradually, once the doctors decided to fish in other places than my legs, my wounds began positively to heal. At the beginning of November, more than three months after being hit, I was told by Hart that I could go on leave for a week and then he would see about releasing me. Naturally I jumped at the chance, for now I would see Madrid. No problem about a companion either. Nils Kruth, an American and a good pal for many weeks, was now fit enough and he too obtained permission for the jaunt.

On 3 November, armed with official passes, we went by train to Terancon and then hitchhiked into Madrid for six wonderful days during which the heavily charged atmosphere of the city, the spirit and courage of the people swept away the oppressive, depressing mood engendered by lengthy hospitalization. Once again I was ready, rather than resigned, to face up to the future. I have referred elsewhere to this visit and will say no more now: Madrid and Madrileños deserve a book to themselves.

To my astonishment and even anger, Hart announced the day after our return that my left leg needed one more "clearing up." In itself this was not serious, but it put back the healing and final signing-off by several days. About now, too, Kruth left. Apart from his friendship I lost his valued assistance in improving my Spanish. His own was excellent and he was a good teacher.

It was late November when I finally escaped from Huete. Bidding farewell to the Spanish staff of Ward D was a sad occasion, for it seemed unlikely we would ever meet again. I liked and respected them all. Ramón, the serious, conscientious ward orderly, unbent sufficiently to hug me, Spanish style. Elderly Candida who, I fear, never saw Bristol again, sighed deeply—"Ah, this war, this war."

Lively Pilar of the flashing eyes and jet black hair laughingly gave me a quick kiss. And from much-loved Anita, a Madrileña, always cheerful, kind and compassionate, the real boss of Ward D, a gentle smile, a firm handshake and her hopes for my future safety. Poor Anita. She married a young wounded German patient soon after I left. Months later I met Ramón again. He told me that Ernst, her husband, went back to the Front. Anita had a baby and died, with her baby, in childbirth, adding yet another grave to the growing number behind the hospital. Writing this brings her vividly to mind and I am sad.

III

December, 1937-January, 1938
The Battle of Teruel

But at last I was back with the Battery. Once again they were in billets in Mondejar, though the month before had seen them in action with the British Battalion.[24]

Many changes in the Battery since I left them. Chiefly for the better. Dunbar, of course, was wounded a day or two after me and since then Hugh Slater has been in command. At the moment though, he and Alan Gilchrist are in hospital with flu and so Otto Estenson is in charge. This seems to suit everybody (it does me too) since Slater is not very popular while we all like Otto.

Both Dunbar and Slater were subsequently promoted and went to Brigade H.Q. Staff. In accordance with Government decree the Battery now had many Spaniards, as did each of the Battalions. I was pleased to find George Baker as cheerful and unflappable as ever, and readily resumed our friendship. Miles Tomalin, now termed rather grandly "Cultural Responsable," took this elevation as one would expect, with a grin.

Miles has his own "house" and has got out an excellent wall-newspaper. By the way, he showed me a snap from Peggy Ashcroft to whom the old No. 1 Gun-crew wrote way back in June asking her to become our "pin-up." There was a friendly message on the back of the photo.

It was at this same "House of Culture" that the coach conveying us old-timers on our 1981 visit stopped when, on a fine afternoon, we went

53

for a drive into the countryside around Madrid. Soon, the name of a village sounded familiar. Then—"To Mondejar."

Just outside the village was Miles' house, and the man himself, frail and white-haired now, beamed like a small boy as, with the rest of us, he clambered down from the coach.

Derelict, minus doors and windows, the house had a special place in the affections of all us Anti-tanks, but to no one did it mean more than to Miles himself. We British volunteers were a very mixed crowd. Miners, bricklayers, carpenters, and so forth, we were, in the main, real working class, even if so many had been long unemployed in those grim 30s. But there were others too: doctors, lecturers, writers, poets, students—intellectuals who shared our understanding of the issues in Spain, and paid as high a price as the rest of us in killed and wounded. Alas, by some of our more aggressive proles such men were regarded with suspicion. For years we had sung, and some even believed, that "The emancipation of the Working Class is the task of the Workers alone" and everyone knew that intellectuals were not workers.

In an inspired moment Authority put Miles in charge of our Battery Culture and Morale. He very quickly proved himself worthy, for he was indeed an artist with both feet firmly on the ground. Outstanding among his contributions to our entertainment and good cheer was a succession of wall-newspapers published—pinned on any convenient wall Miles could find—under the name, "Assault and Battery News." Miles had taken over the groundfloor room of this one-up one-down house into which we now crowded. Here, "A&B News" had flourished. Chatting happily to the BBC crew, Miles stood outside and we all smiled, equally happy to see him reliving what were, surely, some of his finest memories.

With Chris Smith, an erstwhile Anti-tank comrade, I climbed to the room above, so well remembered by us both. But the filth and muck of many years together with unimaginative graffiti did nothing to restore the emotions of those days, and we quickly returned to the sunshine outside.

At a new and brash restaurant on the main road we bought fizzy lemonade, then climbed back into the coach. But we stopped again, though briefly, for a view of the large house, now seemingly occupied and in good repair, which had twice served as 15th Brigade Headquarters. This glimpse brought its memory of a cultural evening spent there, and of another odd man out. Malcolm Dunbar, one of that period's aesthetic set who, by birth, upbringing, and interests would seem an unlikely recruit to our People's Army, became our first Anti-tank Battery Commander. He was, I recalled, promoted full lieutenant on the occasion of our arrival at this same house on our way to the Jarama Front. He came out wearing his new second bar of rank and shyly admitted his advancement, which we all considered well-deserved. Despite his positively aristocratic bearing and deceptively haughty manner, he made the best job possible for him of accepting our uncouth insensitiveness—as it must have seemed to him. By those values by which men are judged in war he was an inspiration to us all. I have never known a braver man; the more to be admired since he was, I am sure, well aware of fear. He died, tragically, several years later.

Looking at the house from our coach windows I saw Dunbar again so clearly, standing with a group of us in the very large groundfloor room, watching a party of ballet dancers performing on an improvised stage. They were from England; more than likely he had himself played a part in their coming to Spain on this supportive visit. Dunbar's face was a study, his obvious pleasure in the performance, the dancers so gracefully whirling away all the dirt and ugliness of war—and the hurt, as he heard the only half-suppressed guffaws and derisory comments from some of the onlookers. No, we were not always, all of us, such good comrades.

Antonio let the clutch out, the coach moved on, and the house slipped away into yesterday.

The 15th Brigade, the British Battalion and we Anti-tanks did not remain long in Mondejar after I rejoined. There was just time for me to settle in again, and in a manner very much to my liking.

2nd December. Miles Tomalin has managed our Paper so well that he has been taken away from our Battery and attached to Brigade to run Our Fight. *I am taking over from him. In fact, my official title now is "Cultural Responsable!"*[25]

3rd December. A political meeting was held in the Battery at which I was the speaker.

How I wish I had kept notes on what I said, or even what was the subject. And, did I dare to attempt my own translation for the benefit of the Spanish comrades now an integral part of our unit?[26] My memory is as blank as my diary on details. I know that my new exalted position was partly due to Arthur Nicoll, then the Battery Political Commissar, who thought well of me. Miles, too, had urged my promotion.

On the Saturday I satisfied myself, at any rate, by an edition of "Assault and Battery News," as well as producing a concert which—

went down pretty well. Miles turned up and praised the newspaper.

By the 7th of December my mail had again adjusted from hospital to Returned to Unit, and cigarettes were in sufficiently good supply to warrant the following:

Got some eggs to-day, the first for a very long time. Managed this by bartering some spare fags (Spanish "pillow-slips").

Then on the 9th we received orders to pack and be ready to move immediately. My cultural post vanished at once and I was, instead, in charge of the ammunition group. We left on six trucks about 3 A.M.. It was to be a long journey. Not until the 16th did we finally reach its end, and the end of rumors as to our destination.

The start was the customary one of traffic snarl-ups and general confusion. Everyone else seemed to be on the move at the same time, wanting the same piece of road. By 8:30 the next morning we and masses of others arrived at Temblaque, that ill-begotten rail junction where, back in June, a combination of intense heat and tummy trouble had left me with extremely unpleasant memories of the place.

10th December. In June this was the hottest railway station I had ever had to hang around in; now it is the coldest. Shipped on board a train into closed boxcars. After much shunting up and down we eventually left about 4pm. It's bitterly cold. Arrived at Albacete (Home for Incurables) about 2am. Not allowed to leave the train. Given coffee and cigarettes. Left on the way to Valencia (we are going to the Aragon Front) about 3am.

11th December. Christ, but it's cold. The sun is shining and it's a lovely day for a walk, a good sharp one, but not for sleeping in wagons. Here we are, stopped, somewhere on the way to Valencia; have been here about two hours. Boiled part of our iron rations into something like a stew, and made some hot coffee, so things are better.

This long, slow travelling seems to me not unlike how it must have been in Russia, soon after 1917. I have read about the stops with every-one going out for hot water to make tea—soldiers, civilians (complete with family and goods) packing the trains and camping in the stations. Here it is just the same. There are hordes of them here, platforms and tracks are strewn with groups of soldiers and civilians, young children and even babies, crouched around fires, with military and civilian gear everywhere. The soldiers seem to have a plentiful supply of coffee which they give to the children—some of them do, anyway. Of course, no one gets real coffee anywhere anymore.

I still think the sight of these families parked in such conditions and in such cold weather is one of the most pitiful I have ever seen.

Day after day and night after night we continued our stop-start journey. The wagon became home to us. Valencia, Tarragona, Reus. Then Hijar, where we thought wrongly that we would leave the train, was reached about 5 A.M. on the 12th.

13th December. The sun is shining and it is beautifully warm when you are able to get out in it during the day. Still at Hijar at 11am. Have read the Bulletin which says there is a great fascist (!) offensive going on in this area. Well, we shall see soon enough.

In fact, I don't believe we heard of it again. Still in our wagons we left Hijar for Alcañiz. There we stayed aboard overnight and early on the 14th unloaded guns, gear, and ourselves and camped in the station.

Apparently we are waiting for camions (trucks), but where we are going to Heaven alone knows. It is very cold now, particularly minus our wagons. I think that of all the memories of Spain and of this war the most vivid and lasting will be these travels. Things often go wrong, but how anybody could organise this mass of humanity and goods as they do beats me.

15th December. Slept in some empty wagons in a siding last night and managed quite a fair sleep. To-day it is again extremely cold and we are still messing around the station.

16th December. Phew, some night. Told definitely not moving until to-day, so George and I organised a comfy bed in a wagon. Roused about

1.30—trucks here. Worked so hard loading up I even got warm. But not for long. Usual smart change-over. Hanging about for God knows what. Then, five miles from our destination, my ammo truck punctured. Took two hours to change the wheel and of course the others went on. Eventually reached the town where we are to be quartered. As I was in charge I went into H.Q. to find the whereabouts of the Battery. Came out, and the bleeding truck had gone!

But (fortunately for me) all was soon well and an hour or so later guns, goods and personnel were reunited in Barracks once again.

This place is called Alcorisa. Still no sign of the War, although I believe we are nearer to the Teruel Front.

Harry Pollitt, General Secretary of the British Communist Party, came to see us on the 17th of December.[27] The Battery culture was again in my hands, although, in view of a summons to move being daily expected, I also remained in charge of ammunition. In the latter role I did what was needed. As far as recreation went, I managed an abbreviated wall newspaper in Pollitt's honour. After his well-received speech the whole Battery joined in a sing-song.

We often had such musical evenings, though usually they were impromptu. They made up a kind of U.K. symposium, adding greatly to my knowledge of obscenity as well as revolutionary prose and poetry! Led by one of our Scots boys we revelled in masochism with "The Ball of Kirriemuir," all verses, and several others of equal appeal if not satisfaction. Generally the Irish were of sterner stuff and we responded with varying degrees of enthusiasm to such amiable sentiments as:[28]

> Oh God curse you England,
> You cruel-hearted monster;
> Your treason would shame
> All the Devils in Hell . . .
> or
> Another martyr for Old Ireland,
> Another murder for the Crown;
> British laws may crush the Irish
> But cannot keep their spirit down . . . .

Wales, ever jealous of its reputation as, first, a land of song and, second, the land with the biggest chip on its shoulder vis à vis English perfidy, could be relied upon to express such sentiments in fair melody, even if "Land of My Fathers" was all the Welsh most of them could manage.

We English were outclassed in the contest for the most oppressed country, but determinedly put the ball back in its rightful court with a rousing—

> Come workers sing a rebel song,
> A song of love and hate;
> Of love unto the lowly
> And of hatred to the great . . . .

Given a sufficiency of vino to work on a natural disposition to depression and pessimism one chap, name forgotten, would give a solemn rendering of "Thora" (well received by Harry Pollitt) and an equally cheerless number which went—

> I would not chide thee,
> Chide thee, Margarite,
> Nor mar one joy of thine so sweet . . . .

Always, of course, "Nellie Dean" made a grand lead-in to the concluding "International."

In the month of December, and as a welcomed correction of the unfounded report of a fascist offensive, the Republic had begun a major attack against the important town of Teruel. Initially this was to be carried out by Spanish troops only. The clear intention was to show other governments that the Spanish Republic was no longer dependent on Internationals. But all International Brigades, like our own 15th, were being brought into this region ready to go if necessary. Not unexpectedly, strong fascist resistance eventually made this vital.

News of the battle came daily. On the 17th we heard that Government troops were fighting in the first houses and had surrounded the city.

December 21st. Apparently definite about Teruel. It's entered anyway. Seems by Spanish troops only, which is a terrific leg-up for the Spanish Army.

Inevitably sometime that day came orders for the Battery to be prepared to move.

Wed. 22nd. Well, last night was Mafeking Night![29] *Teruel is captured, definitely. Grand news. Now we can hope for other things.*

Five days later there was still fierce fighting in Teruel's streets.

Meanwhile we made the best job we could of the Spartan conditions in which we were living. High in the mountains as we now were, the cold was intense. We added any garment obtainable, official or otherwise. Since we all slept in our clothes—as much for warmth as for instant readiness—I don't think we looked over-smart.

Alcorisa had little to offer except cafes in which vino and even cognac were still available. Yet it was a friendly town to us. In an impressive setting, it well repaid with wonderful views the effort involved in climbing the many steep paths and roads around it. One long hike took me up a rough track skirting the town. From below I had seen what looked like caves high in the hillside, and people moving about. The many twists and turns as the path followed the contours of the hill made it a long, hard slog. Eventually, rounding yet another bend, I came upon them, perhaps twenty dug into the hill. By their appearance I guessed them to be gitanos—gypsies. As I drew nearer the women at once disappeared into their houses, taking their children with them. The men stood their ground, unsmiling eyes fixed upon me, not one responding to my greetings. So plainly did they resent my presence I turned back immediately. Could it be, I wondered, that even in Republican Spain gypsies felt vulnerable? At a bend in the path I looked back; the women and children were out again in the winter sunshine as I, the disturber of their seclusion, made my retreat.

Christmas was now very near: the battle for Teruel grew even more fierce. We concentrated on preparations for the former and tried to ignore the implications of the latter. The long, narrow room which served our Anti-tank Battery as dormitory, recreation and general purpose room, was to be our party place for Christmas Day. Our own Battery kitchen was, we understood, scouring the countryside for extras, while the official Commissariat intended to honor the occasion by providing what they could for the festive board. In addition organizations at home, particularly the Communist Party, were sending a parcel to each man with a Christmas pudding, cigarettes, and chocolate! The twenty or so Spanish comrades now members of the Battery, smiled benignly on our efforts and enthusiasm and did what they could to contribute. Needless to say it was unanimously decided without debate that all parcels received would be deemed as sent to the whole. We waited to see which would come first—Christmas, or our move to the Front.

By my own account I worked extremely hard preparing a special Christmas Edition of "Assault and Battery News" as well as writing one short sketch and a monologue, to be performed by a willing cast on the night.

We had our Christmas Day. My edition of "A & B News" was on display from dawn and a concert, including the comic sketch (it could hardly be other than comic) was arranged for the evening. Enough trestle tables were scrounged and placed with seating for us all as well as several guests from Brigade and the British Battalion. (For most of us eating at a table was a rarity. We usually collected our ration and squatted on the ground to eat). On the trestles was a motley collection of tin plates, dixies, biscuit tins, tin bowls, tin mugs, and indeed almost anything which might do service as a container, with not a single piece of china—precious or otherwise—in sight. The cutlery was of a kind. Boxes with a plank across, or just boxes, and one broken chair, made up the seating. The grand feast was to take place at 6oc in the evening.

Saturday, 25th December, 11pm. How we appreciated the wisdom of pooling our cash and sending a truck out on the scrounge to see what could be bought to augment our rations. Here in a small town quite near the Front we sat down—55 of us—to, first, a thin soup of macaroni. It was very good and some ate a little too much on the principle, usually a sound one, that if the first course is good eat a lot of it if available, for God knows what the next will be like. But this time our cooks triumphed. For then came four big turkeys and five chickens, with suitable garnishing!

In due course we had our Christmas pudding and drank our toasts—in champagne! Oddly enough, this was still fairly easy to obtain, though I suspect the quality would not please the connoisseur, a suspicion reinforced by its cheapness.

The evening's concert was enthusiastically received by one and all, their ready appreciation made easier by a good supply of vino, cognac, and vermouth. Genuine peanuts were at hand, and real English cigarettes. My sketch was called, "Trotsky in Madrid." All I can remember of it is of its being a very unsubtle play upon General Quepo de LLano's radio promise of a year before that he would very soon be taking coffee in the Gran Via, Madrid. This never fulfilled boast gave rise to the apocryphal story of the table set permanently for one outside a cafe in that fashionable street and labeled "Reserved": Madrileños, of course, delighted in the General's non-appearance. I also recall George Baker's admirable "Scarlet Woman," but am unable to help even myself as to what each had to do with the other, apart from both being in the same sketch.[30]

Even the most jaundiced among us, and we had some, went to bed happy at about 10:45; to-morrow was just the 26th of December. To the several Scotsmen in our company it was not a bad rehearsal for the real thing they still hoped for—Hogmanay.[31]

26th December. Saw Malcolm Dunbar in town. He had just come back from Teruel where, he said, only a few houses were still holding out and these completely cut off, our line now being some kilometres north of the town. But he told us that their aviation was very active. Again, God help civilians in war-time.

27th December. At last something seems to be afoot. Orders to pack and be ready to move at two hours' notice.

2 P.M. Not yet received word, but all packed and all personnel confined to barracks. One thing I would like—to move in daylight. Improbable.

I find I have not mentioned a few interesting things that have happened to me these last days. First, Brigade H.Q. asked for me to go and assist Miles Tomalin on Our Fight. *Battery chiefs objected, so I'm staying here. Next, Bill Cranston is back from hospital and I'm relieved from being in charge of Ammo. How are the mighty fallen. Most important of all though: Battery chiefs instructed by Brigade to appoint deputies for themselves prior to going into action. Result, Alan Gilchrist appointed second-in-command; in the undesirable event of either Arthur Nicoll or Otto Estenson getting knocked out, I am to be Political Commissar! Most flattering. Meantime, I am still relieved of all guards, fatigues etc., and confess I do not find this unpleasant.*

For three days we awaited the word to go. Cranston returned once more to hospital putting me in charge of ammunition again. Wearing my cultural hat I flirted with the idea of some sort of concert for New

Year's Eve, should we still be around. Apparently my "Trotsky" sketch was a success; anyway, they wanted it again.

Hogmanay still tottered on the brink, and the Scots lads went about with drawn and anxious faces, in no mood for Sassenach frivolity or misplaced humour.

Then the blow fell.

Friday 31st December, 1937. Jesus, what a New Year's Eve! Oh, blimey. Got the order to move at 6.30 this morning. Going up to the Teruel Front. Left Alcorisa about 10 A.M. Travelling right into the mountains, higher and higher and higher, more and more bleak, desolate and deserted. Also, it is snowing heavily. Fed about 2oc on sardines and a piece of chocolate (!). Beautiful scenery, of a kind I have never even imagined before. Terrific heights, winding roads, canyons, peaks and snowdrifts. Still climbing. Bitterly cold.

7 P.M. Brrrh! We seem to have got somewhere. Last few villages blown to hell. We are on a kind of plateau, goodness knows how high. Still snowing heavily. We are a few miles from Teruel. Have stopped at a ramshackle house, one room, half the roof off and one wall down. As we arrived in the half dark the sight of the countryside with its destroyed houses, the complete absence of any sort of civilisation apart from us 50 odd half frozen men, presented a picture of real misery.

Unloaded all five trucks and somehow or other got everything into the house except the guns. Then our cooks made some hot coffee and hard-boiled eggs. No sooner had the trucks gone than orders came from Brigade H.Q. that we were in a dangerous position, too near a village which they apparently bomb frequently, and would have to move out! Then the fun really started; fierce snowstorm, everything freezing fast, us sliding about in the pitch darkness carrying boxes of ammunition. The trucks returned and we loaded up again. Then "they" simply ordered us to take the trucks about a mile away and sleep on them. Jesus.

So here we are now at about five minutes to midnight, lying in open trucks covered with snow, stores and men freezing rapidly.

Happy New Year!

So we saw the New Year in. George Baker, never one to be easily put out, improvised a canopy of sorts for two and a small piece of candle, both of which lasted just into 1938. After that we resigned ourselves to a most unpleasant night.

As the scene of a battle in which the 15th Brigade had played a major part, Teruel was, of course, high on the list of our "Return to the Battlefields" tour of 1981. To the hazards of war, the maiming and killing, were added cold so intense that few of us had ever experienced anything so bad before, except perhaps some of the Scots, general and varied hardships such as inadequacies of food and clothing, all combining to attach a special grimness to the very name, Teruel.

But now our luxury coach took us comfortably to the town and a satisfactory hotel. The day was wet and cold. Despite some fine days we were not getting the constant warm sunshine of late Spring that I had promised my wife was usual. Though to me the grey skies and lowering clouds seemed fitting; few had other than bleak memories of the place.

Exploring the town, we entered the Cathedral, dark and over-solemn, then were allowed in to a nearby house to see the famous, centuries old, "Two Lovers," imprisoned in their glass tomb, clasping hands, a grisly affirmation of true love.[32] Not unexpectedly, in the Town Square was a larger than life bust of Franco; it gazed down on us rather more benignly than its original would have done. . . .

Aided perhaps by the continuing bad weather we were all a little depressed by Teruel, despite the friendly welcome from some local people. After all, it was another town which, apart from its temporary capture by the Republic in December 1937, had been in Franco's hands almost from the beginning of the war. There must be many older people still living who had suffered dreadfully during those ghastly winter months of its being first attacked by our forces and its eventual recapture by the fascists; nor would they all have been fascists.

Next day, before we resumed our tour, local comrades took us a mile or so out of town. There, by the roadside, they showed us a recently erected simple monument:

To the 1005 men and women of Teruel shot by the fascists, August 1936.

As our coach sped away and I looked up at the cloud-covered hills, my thoughts returned to that truck parked in deep snow on a road not so far away, on New Year's Eve, 1937.

Saturday, 1st January, 1938. Good job I'm a cheerful sort of guy. Never been so cold in all my life as I was last night. George and I spent most of it running up and down the road, snow-storm and all. Temperature last night was 20 below zero, which is going some for me.

Still snowing like hell. Managed to get some coffee and more sardines about 7oc this morning. Supposed to be going somewhere else soon but in the meantime are digging foxholes in case of avion. About 3 kilometres behind the line.

The rest of that day and the next we spent aimlessly as far as our war effort was concerned. Individually we concentrated on the desperate necessity not so much of getting warm as of preventing freezing. Our efforts to this end were not aided by frequent dashes into nearby snow-filled ditches whenever enemy aircraft came over. Orders and counter orders came thick and fast from Brigade.

3rd January. Left Argente just as dark came on last night. Hell of a trip. Trucks went off the road into a four feet deep snowdrift and we had to get them out. Arrived at another damned village around 9 P.M. Stayed around in the snow until H.Q. decided what to do with us. Finally slept in a barn. We have had three of our lot conk out with the cold. By the way, the name of this pleasant little place is—Fuentes Calientes, which in English means, "Warm Springs!"

Later. Now at Rillo, in another barn, but expect to go up in the hills as the British Battalion has done, for apparently we are near the line here and are forming another temporary one just in case. We left one gun back at Argente to support the Mac-Paps (Canadian) Battalion.

Later still. No move to-night. Scouts came back and reported hills impassable by night—snow goodness knows how deep. Glad to say I'm back with a gun crew again, Cranston being out of hospital. Had our first hot meal to-night for three days. Had been having sardines and bread. Good job I like sardines.

By the way, I washed to-day—in snow.

4th January. We, No. 2 Gun, went up that hill early this morning. Found it was a bloody mountain, not a hill. Waist deep in snow, the ground, when you find it, all rock.

Later. Atta boy! Order to move out, fascists cutting us off! And this with hearing only a few rounds of machine-gun fire all day. Now waiting, with loaded trucks, back in village for further orders.

5th January. Went to sleep fairly comfortably last night in the barn. Of course they had to keep the game going by rousing us all at 3 A.M and telling us to wait for further orders. It's a great life. Got us up again at 6oc. No. 1 Gun loading up now to go some other place. We, No. 2 Gun, stay hanging around for yet more orders. They have properly split the Battery now. As to the fascists cutting us off yesterday, that seems to have been the usual sort of blurb.

Last night and to-day I swear the temperature is a lot lower than 20 below. And the nice hot supper we were looking forward to did not materialise through a lousy trick on the part of the British Battalion Quartermaster who refused to serve us. By the time we got an order over his head the grub had been finished. This is all through being split up— they have decided to take away our own kitchen for the time being.

Later. No orders for us until after midday when somebody seemed to think it would be a good idea for us (No. 2 Gun) to take up the same position as before. Since there did not appear to be any great hurry, and it was already past 3oc, our Political Commissar decided to put it off until to-morrow morning. Suits us. So we organised things and got a really big fire going in our barn. I am warm now for the first time in about six days—really warm, I mean.

6th January. Well, it's a good job we didn't take that order too literally yesterday. Just turning in last night when new orders came to load up immediately. Fortunately, knew enough to make a few enquiries from H.Q. first. Since they had neglected to send trucks, this was very necessary anyway! Orders amended to "Stand-by." Went back to sleep and left a double guard. Woken up again about midnight: "Trucks on the way, load up." Still stayed in bed—we know those trucks. This morning at 10 am trucks still had not come.

I was sent off to a little village called Orris to get stores, since we have decided to start our own kitchen again. When I got back they were loading up, trucks having eventually arrived. We had some food (more sardine) and left about 12.30. Now, at 2.30, we seem to have reached our destination. We are nearer to Teruel but exactly where I cannot say.

There is heavy artillery banging away and every sign of the war being bloody near. Waiting for more orders.

The Battle of Brunete saw the finish of the "heroic" phase of my diary keeping. It remained to the very last word naive, coy and very proper; but the realities of war, especially contrasted with the relative picnic of our own particular experience of the post-battle Jarama Front, brought home to me the inadequacy of some of my pious platitudes of earlier days.

After Brunete came hospital for a long time, and that I regard as my "cynical" period. Teruel undoubtedly saw my "moaning" session!

Most of us moaned, groused, and grumbled at most times and in most places. Living as we were this was as natural as breathing—and nearly as necessary. The majority of this niggling was accepted as little more than conversation, to which one listened with whatever patience could be managed and then added one's own contribution. A few irredeemably bad-tempered souls came readily to mind, but even more easily I recall those many stalwarts who could always be relied upon to offer encouragement and even a joke, or at least not to add to one's own perhaps depressed mood by a single word.

I was fortunate on two counts. First, since I had rejoined the Battery at Ambite, George Baker and I had resumed the close comradeship of our beginning. And George, if undemonstrative, was almost completely unflappable. I don't recall his ever merely grousing. If he at last decided that somebody's behavior had become intolerable, he told the culprit so in plain terms and that was that. George was a tower of strength to me, and not only in digging our dugouts! My other advantage was in the assiduous keeping of my diaries. Whatever might be their value as a true and correct record, they were the means by which I indulged my moods, my depressions, my fears and hopes—myself. So, generally, I moaned to the scribbled page rather than to my mates. This spared them and helped me.

7th January. No more orders last night so tried to sleep on the trucks. I think it was even worse than the other time. "Cold" is a silly, futile word, absolutely inadequate. Anyway, it's gone, and though to-night may be worse—still, we can't have last night over again: logic!

This morning I played at Quartermaster again to Orris. Lots of avion, artillery and machine-gun fire now. Got back and found my gun had gone up the hill (mountain), behind three mules. Trailed after it, caught up at the top and found the elevation of the gun had gone wrong. We were supposed to be supporting the Mac-Paps, but could not get the gun right so had to come down the mountain again. Now waiting at the roadside for orders.

It's about 8 days now since I washed! It isn't because you don't want to, it's simply that you can't. The name of this village appears to be Labradas, or something like that. The fascists are pushing in the Perales-Alcaniz sector.

8th January. (With the gun still out of action). This morning I was sent off to locate Otto Estenson's gun, which is supporting the Lincoln-Washington (American) Battalion. What a trek. Miles and miles up into the mountains, incidentally providing some of the most majestic scenery I have ever imagined, for about 10 kilometres. Went up with a mule cart which was taking up ammunition. Two scouts from the Lincoln took us, and guided us over the brow of a hill. The sight of three mules, a cart, and half a dozen men was too tempting for the fascists, who opened fire on us. I am very proud of the fact that one of the scouts and I were the only ones to keep our nerve and our heads and get that cart unloaded before any damage was done or anyone hit.

And should anyone wonder why bother to unload the cart when it could have been moved back, mules and all, I can only ask—have you ever tried moving mules? Whether they disliked the view from the other side of the hill or were responding to the shouts and snarls of their drivers, I don't know, but eventually one turned, his mates followed, and we loaded up again and went on our way—making sure we kept out of sight.

Found Otto. They have already been in action. Not too good a position, and food—which is being supplied by the American Battalion—pretty lousy. Otto asked if we could supply more grub.

Got back about 2.30, found my own gun now O.K. and ready to move off to join the Mac-Paps. Had some food, then climbed the bloody mountain again with them. The Mac-Paps and us are in a kind of second-line position, while the Lincoln-Washingtons are in the front and well over to the right. Climbed this time, I suppose, perhaps six or seven kilometres. Got down to it and dug in with George. Had grub from the Mac-Paps. No. 3 Gun has gone over to the left, supporting the 24th, Spanish Battalion, so we are once more a well-split Battery.

*10th January. We are moving the gun into another position to-day, on
to a small flat stretch. This action seems to be going well for us. Teruel is
definitely finished for the fascists, and all their attacks here trying to cut
the road have been repulsed. Now our Army may make a further attack,
seeing that their counter-attack seems to have been smashed. All of
which is pretty good.*

Oh dear! At the time I made no note of who or what prompted this
optimistic assessment. It might have been that although all three guns had
spent a week belting up and down mountains into and out of positions in
a general atmosphere of excitement if not order, only one gun had so far
fired in anger. Or, of course, it was possibly the result of Political
Commissars at mere Battery level having not much more idea of the true
facts than had we gun-crews.

The most likely cause could well have been a rush of blood to my head
following an improvement in our food supply when our own kitchen
became operative again. This happening brought honorable mention in
my diary, though.

*But by the time they've brought the food to us, four or five miles, it is
absolutely cold. Still, can't be helped.*

Unmitigated joy, however, at the day's end:

Very well off for English and American fags these days, God knows why.

Still I had not managed a wash; no water, and the snow gone for the
time being.

Nowadays, I believe, every good general insists upon every man under
his command being put in the picture before battle commences. But I'll
bet that clarity of intention and method didn't last long once the guns—
theirs as well as ours—opened up and battalions, companies, platoons,
and even individuals were soon scurrying here and there as, amid growing
chaos, the enemy persisted in playing to their own rules, not yours.

On those occasions when I could say I knew what was happening in
my near vicinity, I felt quite chuffed. As to knowing with any accuracy
the general development of a battle, we usually discovered this when it
was over. I like to think that somebody near the top had some idea but I

can't help believing that it didn't trickle down very far. By and large
Political Commissars, well-meaning fellows, either passed on what scraps
they were themselves fed, or indulged themselves and us in platitudes. To
be honest, few of us found this lacking in usefulness or appeal: after the
first days of initial success, an accurate assessment of the state of battle
might well have been less welcome than the common belief that we were
doing all right.

Recent years have produced many accounts of the Civil War by fellow
International Brigaders. Time after time I have read with awe the wealth of
detail, the precision, the confident assertions brooking no questioning, the
facts culled from memories of events and incidents of thirty, forty, or even
fifty years earlier. And not one of them kept anything like even the modest
personal account which I managed. Faced with such powers of observation, such capacity for total recall and seeming omniscience, my humility
is complete. In excuse for my ignorance I can say only that those same
people, when my companions of those days, gave little evidence of being
any more aware than was I.

So it is by benefit of hindsight alone that I now see the efforts of the
Republic to capture and hold Teruel were doomed from the start of the
campaign. Perhaps, like other Government offensives, it had to be
attempted. It did thwart Franco's plans for a time. And, of course, there
was a remote chance of success; Franco could and did make errors of
judgement, his allies, especially the Italians, not always being obedient to
his wishes. Then, too, almost incredibly in view of the crushing losses in
men and material ultimately suffered by the Republic, it was beyond doubt
a great morale boost: Spanish troops, unaided by the Internationals, had
captured the town. Quite rightly this achievement was much lauded by all
of us. I suppose some wideawake (or plain cynical) people noted that
almost as the last houses fell to our troops all the International Brigades
were rushed in to begin the dreadful task of holding on. But lack of sufficient trained troops and the absence of vital arms and planes, finally
defeated even the bravest, fighting as they were in appalling conditions,
always cold, often hungry, but never despairing.

One important and relevant point rarely referred to is the quality, military professionalism, of our officers. It seems almost as though the fact of
being such in the International Brigade was itself a guarantee of soldierly
skills.

How well were we led? If personal bravery and disregard for their own
safety count (as of course they do) then I would say superbly. But I think

it not unfair to suggest that military expertise was too often sadly lacking—at any rate, inadequate to the gigantic tasks before them. In the sometimes arbitrary, even whimsical, promotions which occurred—many politically motivated, some resulting from dire necessity during a battle—it was inevitable that there would be misfits. Few failed to lead their men bravely, but courage alone is a heady draught; too often it was not enough.

Quite early in January the fascist counter offensive at Teruel had already achieved some success and, more alarming to our High Command, was gaining impetus daily as their strength on the ground increased and their planes swept largely unchallenged through the skies. But we in the ranks knew little of this. Food and the freezing temperature occupied my thoughts and took their unworthy place in my account.

12th January. Some improvement in the food situation to-day, following our own Battery kitchen operating once more. Heavy snow again in the night.

13th January. Tolerable night last night, except for guard duty; lousy night for that. Heavy mist came up in the early hours, soaking everything. Still hanging about, no chance of putting anything out to dry, nowhere to sit down, and inches of mud for walking in. Definitely unpleasant. By the way, I produced a special, single-sheet newspaper yesterday.

This, like all our "Battery News," was, of course, hand-written. I remember Alan Gilchrist praising my effort and taking it with him for the enlightenment and uplift of the other gun-crews!

We moved again next day.

14th January. Mid-day. In a field somewhere or other, about 4 kilometres from Teruel. What is happening nobody seems to know exactly. The Front, judging by the noise, is not far away. We have moved the gun away from some nearby buildings and are awaiting orders. This looks like the real thing again, their avion, I mean.

Sod it! The last half hour was definitely unpleasant. The bastards shelled us, the first I've had really near me for a long time and I did not enjoy it. A hectic battle raging all along the Front now. We move up into position to-night. Had a real wash to-day—found a stream. That apart, to-day reminds me unpleasantly of Brunete.

15th January. Well, we moved yet again last night, and what a move! First, a truck pulled us (No. 2 Gun) about 5 kilometres up the mountain. The track was of course terrible and we nearly turned over several times. Then we unloaded everything and commenced the pull of another 4 kilometres. We had to go up the peaks and down the valleys, using planks to cross one wide stream, three trenches and one small canyon about 30 feet deep. Boy, what a position for a quick getaway! Eventually we arrived at the H.Q. of the Mac-Paps. This is the Front Line here. Plenty of activity, and trench mortars testify to the closeness of the enemy lines. We are hanging around dugouts, the old fascists' once, I think. Anyway, there are plenty of them.

We are to go up on to the crest, but cannot do that before dark. Food supply went astray this morning. Feeding with the Mac-Paps now; night and morning only, for trucks cannot come higher than where we unloaded last night—road impassible and under fire anyway. George and I went down at 4.30 this morning to collect our ration but, as I said, things went wrong, so we'll have to go without.

It is beautifully warm now! Sitting on sandbags, watching the stream which runs through the valley down below. This could be a pretty spot. They are shelling heavily now but all, so far, going over our heads to the rear; hope they keep on doing so.

Sunday, 16th January. A bright day after another freezing night. Have dug a place for the gun, working till the early hours this morning. Getting very little sleep these nights. Decided to pull the gun up to the position just now (10am) with the aid of 20 or so chaps from the Mac-Paps (and By God we'll need them) but were ordered to wait till dark. I wish we could have got it over and done with. It is certainly going to be a tough job. Our prepared position is right on the top of the crest, about ten yards behind the front trenches, and to get to it we have to go sheer up the face of the rock. And if it's hard going to get it there, it seems to me the only way of bringing it down will be to let it roll! We are certainly in some hectic position this time; with trench-mortars falling around and no place to shelter, it's not healthy.

Can see Teruel quite plainly from our position, not so far away as I thought, about 3 kilometres. Shelling from the fascist lines. Their avion just coming over and our 'Anti' batteries opening up on them. You can't sleep day or night, curse it. But we have found a dugout, which helps.

Maybe it's a good job we were not half way up the crest, with 30 or more chaps at the gun.

Later. Who said England's climate was erratic? This afternoon George and I went down to the river (Alfambra) and had a real, all-over wash! And it was glorious. Afterwards we sat on a bank in the sun, and with their artillery and avion quiet for a while, and a miniature waterfall muting the rifles and machine-guns, it could have been (or almost!) a typical peaceful Sunday afternoon. We might have been sitting by the river at Harlow, Essex, debating whether to go to the "Queen's Head" or the "Forest View" for tea. However, 7 fascist Junkers came over and effectively dispelled the illusion. At the moment they are shelling heavily again and appear to be trying for a house nearby.

Later still. If I ever do get home again, somebody is going to hear all about to-day, from first moment to last!

I find I made similar threats from time to time. To my relief, and even more to that of the potential victims, I can cross my heart and say they were never carried out. Possibly because it became increasingly difficult to differentiate between the horrors of one day and so many others.

17th January. At the moment I am watching, from the crest by our gun, the biggest artillery barrage and most intense and longest air-raid I have seen so far in this war. It began about 7oc this morning when their heavy guns opened up. After shelling more or less indiscriminately for an hour or so, they concentrated everything on a small crest to our right. At the same time, judging by the sound of rifle and machine-gun fire, their troops began a fierce attack in that area, which is still going on at 3 P.M. A thick black pall of smoke hangs over the surrounding crests. They probably have more artillery here than at Brunete, and that beat all records for this war. Twenty odd of their bombers and twice as many chasers are giving us some unpleasant moments, but are also concentrating on the same hill to our right. God knows what it must be like there. The whole damned ground is shaking; ever since they first came over they have been circling round and round, bombing, bombing, bombing. By now, of course, we are quite used to the superiority in numbers anyway of their planes, but even our "Anti" batteries have shut up, so they are having it all their own way. Cannot quite see what is happening on the attacked sector. Somehow or other we merely take it for granted that our lines will hold.

Last night, with the aid of 20 men from the Labor Corp, we pulled our gun up here.[33] We have been trying to dig some sort of shelter for ourselves, but what with avion, shells and trench-mortars we are not making much headway. I suppose it means more "night-shift" for us.

Jesus! There won't be any crest left soon. Thought we also saw tanks moving forward; probably out of our sector, though, or we would be ordered to move over. A Spanish Brigade is holding that crest and they have their own Anti-tank Battery.

18th January. Yesterday late afternoon more trench-mortars came over and gave us a nasty time. The battle on the crest waxed even fiercer and then died down. We thought that was all the excitement for one day but then there were yet more mortars and this time all around us. One came right on top of the gun-pit we had been digging and caved it in. Seeing our pit spoiled like that nearly finished us, after putting in such hard graft digging and collecting timbers. This is a bloody fool position anyway.

They are expecting an attack so we all have to stay right by the gun day and night. The fascists are rumoured to have captured two crests over where the battle was yesterday—and, by the way, it was where we were a few days ago, in front of Labrados.

Later. Well, George and I are dug in now. Their avion has been over several times but no damage to us. Their artillery is going strong on another crest now, in front of yesterday's, so maybe they did capture it. Our heavy guns are replying. Rumours of departure from here soon, owing to this new advance which is supposed to be threatening us with a cut-off. Again?

Major Smith, Mac-Paps Commander, wanted us to fire on fascist trenches this morning.[34] Our Battery Political Commissar, who happened to be with us at the time, told him to get higher authority first, for that would be sheer madness. There is only one place we can fire from—on top of the line. We are here for tanks, and if they come we take the risk, that's all; but to invite trouble, well . . . . Those guys know nothing about the way our guns should be used. Nobody but a fool would have made us bring them up this mountain anyway.

There is definitely some truth in the rumour of a small fascist advance, for no food came up till about 8.30 P.M owing to their now being much nearer the road Alcaniz-Perales-Teruel, and shelling it heavily. If they could break this they would be a big step nearer retaking Teruel; but I don't think they will break it.

About which, now, I can only say at least that last remark shows I was not a defeatist!

19th January. Dull and bitterly cold again to-day and of course the nights are always freezing. Teruel must be the most hectic battle of the war so far, it has lasted since the 13th of December and certainly shows no sign of ending yet. This damned position is getting too hot for our liking. There is now no doubt the fascists have broken through on our right, in the valley. But the line is very complex. We have been standing-to since 3oc as, obviously, a really big push would have to be regarded in the same light as a tank attack. Lines of men can be seen running back from the valley, and two small hills at our end are suddenly spurting fire towards our rear. Now, they won't let us fire! It is dark now but the gun is in position and ready for firing on those hills. In my opinion a minor "scram" is taking place over there.

No food to-day, the truck can't make it. We had a lousy time this afternoon from artillery fire and mortars. Our No. 3 Gun fired from the ridge and brought really big stuff on to themselves.

20th January. What a night! Roused out at midnight and told we were moving. Going to the ridge at the back, same as No. 3 Gun, but to get there we have to cross the river and to do that we must go back to the place where we were on Friday the 14th, that is to say, the bottom of the mountain. We had to pull the gun ourselves the whole way, apart from first getting it down from that crest, for which we had to have help. We did have a mule, but it was so weak we had to pull that as well. At the foot of the mountain we got on to the main Teruel road. By 6oc this morning we had reached the back of the crest, still on the road, and that's where we are at the moment. Just what happens next we don't know. They are shelling us, and we are sheltering in some very good old dugouts of theirs. There was definitely a retreat yesterday. The 216 Brigade broke and gave way under heavy shelling. The British Battalion appears to have gone over there.

Fine to-day, and warmer, but still have had no food by mid-day. However, I think our own kitchen is going to feed us. Had three letters to-day; no chance of writing yet—as much as I can do to scribble this.

21st January. Another bloody all-night session. No damned food all day until 7 p.m. and then out working hard all night. Had to go first to

previous position and collect God knows how many hundreds of shells.
Brought them back and then took the gun along the main road towards
Teruel. Turned off right (in daylight you use a trench) and pulled up for
another kilometre or so to the top of the height. Put the gun in position
literally on top of the front-line trench, and by the time we had brought
the ammunition up it was daylight. We are in a very commanding posi-
tion here, covering those two small hills.

Lots more artillery and avion yesterday. The British and Mac-Paps are
reported to have had a bad time. I do not think this battle, although
longer than Brunete, is as fierce, with the exception of the first day of this
later flare-up, and that hour or so in the evening of the second or third
day. (Whatever it was that happened then was probably the cause of my
threats to tell the world!) Their artillery is certainly hectic, but at Brunete
we had to face that too, and everyday their planes came over as strongly
as the worst day here. Also, then, the bloody war often went on at night.
Here, with one exception, they obligingly call it off at dark—the only
point is, you never know for sure! One other difference of course was the
searing heat then and the freezing cold now. We are in trenches here, but
they are nowhere near as good as those at Jarama; we've found dugouts
though, thank the Lord. Brigade Machine-gun Company is in the line
here, including Danny Doyle, once of Well Street Bookshop, and Harry
Fraser of Hackney. Artillery annoyed us this afternoon, but it is obvious
they have not spotted the gun yet.

22nd January. Slept, thank God, for seven hours, broken of course by
1^1/$_2$ hours guard duty. We are keeping close observation on the fascists'
positions, as well as a rather interesting trench apparently shared by
them and us! Good bit of artillery and avion to-day, but the battle on the
crests seems to have died down.

Well, we have just had a very nasty half hour. About 4.30 we sent
over 20 shells on to the hill in front of us, and of course enjoyed it.
However, then their "75s", a much bigger gun, had us bang in sight, and
oh boy! The bloody things came—1-2-3-4: 1-2-3-4, for half an hour, hit-
ting everywhere except the actual gun. By a sheer stroke of luck there
were no casualties, but you feel like a wet rag after that sort of experi-
ence. If we had tried to keep firing there would have been no gun-crew
left. Everything covered now by a foot or so of earth and debris, as were
we also at times, and has to be dug out.

23rd January. Very little sleep again last night as we were repairing the parapet and digging out the trenches. However, slept in relays a little this morning and feel better. They are shelling us again at the moment and coming unpleasantly close although not, so far, with that devastating accuracy which they showed last night. So maybe it's the usual afternoon shelling. It is just possible that by the repairs we carried out last night we kidded them into thinking the gun is shifted. We are not banking on that.

There are more Spanish troops in the line here now, and not nearly enough dug-outs. Last night they had a bad time trying to sleep on the floor of the trench (and being trodden on) or standing up, leaning against the parapet, and all sorts of weird positions. It was extremely cold, and as I went on guard one chap was crying like a baby.

24th January. It seems the battle for the crests is over, with a partial victory for the fascists, obtained at the loss of many men. Our side too has had its losses and in our Brigade the British and the Mac-Paps have had a bad time. We, as a Battery, have so far been phenomenally lucky. If only the 216 Battalion (Battalion, not Brigade; I do not know which Brigade it is, not ours, anyway) had held out. Their retreat, it seems, was not expected by our side for a moment, hence nothing could be done until too late and the fascists had walked right in.

For a change our avion has been over and bombed behind their lines. Also two "dog-fights." One plane came down behind our lines and another behind theirs, but we were unable to tell whose they were. Rumours of the day: We, the 15th Brigade, are being withdrawn very soon and we, The Republican Army, are pressing heavily at Guadalarama and at Huesca.

George Baker has gone into hospital with kidney trouble. Still the Battery has miraculously had no wounded, but the number of sick has increased to ten.

Later. Well, the ruddy battle may be over, though I doubt it, but the shelling isn't! Started at 2oc to-day, two hours earlier than usual, and was almost as accurate as the other day after we had fired. I defy anybody to stand up to this without feeling it.

Very much to my selfish pleasure, George Baker's respite was brief and he returned from hospital in a few days.

25th January. We had a really good night's sleep last night. It happened this way. When we left our previous position with the Mac-Paps we left 100 anti-tank shells there. And because we don't fire every time the Macs want us to, they don't like us any more. The day we did fire they phoned to say, "You'll fire for the bloody English but not for us!" And last night they sent a message that unless we collected the shells pronto they would dump them. So it looked like another night's work. We would have to go down the cliff in front of us and up the crest on our left, since the mountain road by which we had gone up and down before is now fascist. The route would be impossible for mules, so we would then have to go in a half circle into Teruel. All of which would take a hell of a time. So we were not a little pleased when Chris Smith, our Sergeant in charge, said he would go with the munitions chaps. Of course, it left one fly in the ointment—there were only five of us left to do a night's guard. We arranged this, one hour apiece from midnight to 5am. But how could you expect a chap to wake up at midnight of his own accord to start things off? So we all slept soundly and had no guard! Luckily, nothing happened.

Artillery already started at 11am, and some of ours are replying from somewhere. We are all getting stiff necks from constant bending, particularly since snipers got two Spanish boys near our gun position. Sorry to report that washing is off again since we came up her, no water.

Later. Well, they have certainly given us a bad day. All day long without a break they have been shelling us. One landed right in the trench a few yards away, killing one Spaniard, wounding two. It is now dark. All of us breathe a deep sigh of relief when darkness comes and we find ourselves still alive and kicking. No. 3 Gun also report heavy shelling—some of them seem to be feeling the strain. After I came back from hospital the boys told me there had been nothing like Brunete since. This may not be quite as bad, but by Christ it's a good second! Cheery moment; had a letter from Jean.

26th January. Orders this morning to fire on fascist position. Fired 20 rounds (two boxes less to carry down!) and, very strange and suspicious, we have been waiting half an hour for a reply.

Later. At 4.45 we have just had proof that their battery of guns is still there. But why, until then, they allowed us to have such a quiet day and why, when they did start, they gave us such a general shelling not concentrated on our gun, I can't imagine.

By the way, I forgot to mention that last night we saw the Northern Lights. It was the first time ever for me, and it was indeed beautiful. Took advantage of the relative quiet day to write 9 letters; four more outstanding.

27th January. Very cold and miserable to-day. No sun, rain this morning. The Battle appears to have opened up again, but well over to our right, where they say we are attacking because the fascists have got a little too near the road for comfort. This has been our quietest day so far. It need have been, for with a couple of snowstorms in the late afternoon things were miserable enough.

28th January. Weather much the same as yesterday. Things are quiet again. George Baker returned last night, so we found another dugout between us. I am in it now, trying to get warm, while George is on guard. He tells me Teruel is in a shocking mess from the shelling and fighting which took place during and since its capture.

You can always tell when a campaign is having its effect on chaps—they begin to get on each other's nerves. That is happening with a few here, plus one or two who are showing definite signs of cracking. It certainly has been a tough time, what with the weather, messing around, insufficient sleep, inadequate and wrong kinds of food and last but most certainly not least, the shelling and avion. Some of the No. 3 Gun crew also appear to be feeling it. There is discontent in the Battery at present against Arthur Nicoll. He was Political Commissar, with Otto Estenson as Acting Commander until a few days ago, when Arthur, as superior officer, appointed himself as Commander with Otto second-in-command and Alan Gilchrist as Political Commissar. The query is—why was not Otto given a chance to prove himself? Arthur was all right as P.C., but he can't compare with Otto for knowledge of the guns etc.

Later. Have just written six letters—that about puts me on par again. The battle over to our right is continuing and we are supposed to be having some success. A more or less quiet day for us so far. It's obvious that something must be happening in other places to have caused the fascists to withdraw artillery and avion from here as they apparently have done.

At about 4 A.M. the next day, George and I set off on the long trek back to the road to collect the day's food for our gun crew. It was freezing hard again and in the darkness we slithered and stumbled along, carrying the empties. George dropped a container and the clatter brought curses on our heads from Spanish comrades reluctant to attract fascist attention. The narrow, zig-zagging trenches, occupied by sentries frenziedly flapping their arms about, jumping up and down, suddenly darting off for a few yards, stopping abruptly and charging back at full speed—doing almost anything in fact to prevent freezing at their posts—made slow progress. Here and there some poor fellow was squatting or leaning against the trench wall or even lying on the ground, trying to sleep. In doing our best to avoid these bodies we were, I'm afraid, concerned less with their comfort than with their loaded rifles we might so easily trigger off! At last we were able to break cover and tramped across the frozen ground to our rendezvous with the kitchen truck. We swapped gossip with the lads and filled our four large containers, one of coffee, three of stew. Several small loaves we stuffed into our pockets. The British Battalion had had a bad day they told us; then: "Make sure someone is here between 7 and 8 o'clock to-night." We started back.

The first signs of the bleak January day to come were visible by the time we reached the first trenches once more. Here we agreed to risk the occasional bullet which zipped and whined its way from the fascist lines rather than, encumbered as we now were, endure the hazards and tortuous progress through the trenches. We stayed on top. How wrong we were! All went well until we stopped to rest our arms, for the containers were heavy. One moment I was standing breathing hard from the exertion, the next I was flat on my back and, so they told me afterwards, yelling loudly enough to give comfort and cheer to all enemy within a couple of miles. Stew, coffee and bread—the lot was soon scattered and trodden into the ground. George ran to my aid though, as became a good soldier, not before carefully placing his load out of harm's way—only to find later that the lot had been snaffled by the occupants of the trench into which I was dragged. By the time I was removed on a stretcher it was daylight and too late to attempt to retrieve the situation. Our guncrew, hearing the news later from George, deplored my ill-luck in once again copping one, but regretted even more, I suspect, the complete loss of their day's food.

So, for the second time, I departed from the battle scene prematurely. This time I had a bullet through my left wrist, breaking it, and another through my—yes, here we go again, through my buttock, its exit being dangerously close to but just missing the rectum.

Eventually, feeling very sorry for myself, I was carted off and at last got into Teruel. I stayed in a house of some sort being used as a field hospital, for just as long as daylight lasted. Then they took me back to another makeshift hospital, though where that was I had no idea, nor could I be bothered to ask.

IV

February-May, 1938
From Teruel to the Ebro

Whatever revolutionary ardor was left in me evaporated rapidly during that ride in the ambulance. For several hours, mostly in the dark, as we bumped along the rough roads and rougher tracks, I tried to keep on my right side of the narrow bunk. But my curses were many and varied as, too frequently, I was thrown around, falling on my back so that I yelled with the pain from my backside or, worse still, came down on my left side and the ill-fitting splint on my arm fell off. I was most unhappy.

There were three of us. A young Spanish comrade lay motionless on the lower bunk opposite me, another squatted on the upper berth. One of my involuntary bounces brought my face a foot or so from the lad below, and at once I determined that if it was too much to expect me to forego my self-pity, I wouldn't let it be so very obvious. Faced with the dreadful stomach wound of my companion, I could at least try to suffer in silence—or as near to that as was reasonable in the circumstances. Above, the somewhat older man, a bullet through the calf of one leg, sat shivering with cold as he clutched a blanket close to him. A grimy sock on one foot and a bandage around his wound were all the clothes he had.

No orderly rode with us. They had tied webbing around the badly hurt younger man, knowing he was incapable of saving himself from the effects of the bouncing, swaying vehicle. The wide swathes of bandages around his middle became frighteningly dyed red over a steadily increasing area. His eyes were closed and his breathing came in short gasps. I could not get to the partition separating us from the driver's cab so, with what urgency I could put into my Spanish, I asked the other man to bang hard. He did so, and we stopped. The driver came back, opened the rear door and demanded "Que pasa?"

We pointed to the lower bunk. He climbed in and looked closely at the white face, lifted an eyelid. I said "He's bleeding badly. Can't you do something?"

Making some pretense of adjusting the bandages he answered kindly enough "I'll drive as carefully as I can. We are near the hospital." Then with a cheery encouragement to us he returned to his cab and we were away again. I did not need to be told the lad was dead.

Eventually I reached Benicasim and began another session of half-living. My left arm was put in plaster from hand to shoulder and my buttocks in swaddling clothes. The hospital organisation was not good, the treatment erratic; certainly it was no Huete, no English Hospital. I was in one of the many villas, one-time homes of the wealthy.

It is right on the shore. The sea looks lovely and there are palm trees along the Esplanade. I am looking forward to getting out and seeing it all. But it is not a good hospital. The chicas are overworked, the food is poor and insufficient. I can get nothing to read. My villa is the "Alvarez del Vayo." All, apparently, are named likewise—the "Thaalman," and "Azaña," etc. The whole lot comprise one huge hospital.[35]

On 11 February I was allowed out of bed for one hour, but this resulted in not a little alarm and even some despondency, for the inexpertly applied dressings and bandages around my rear were soon trailing my ankles! The same day brought a visit from a British Labour Party delegation.

The chief point in their favor was that they gave me 20 Woodbines.

The hierarchy of the hospital seemed largely German. As was so frequently the case, the lower orders were reserved for the Spanish—cheerful, hardworking but regrettably not all skilled in the art of applying bandages for the three or more days required of them.

Mostly convalescent, my fellow patients often sorely tried my low-ebb spirits, making me from time to time let loose some uncomradely invective. But, invariably, the chief culprits of the previous night's noisy fun and games, lively Spanish youngsters, would greet me next morning with sincerely expressed condolences on the continuing unsatisfactory state of my backside as evidenced by the running commentary given them by the nurse as she removed the bloody bandages. Their exclamations of sympathy were so patently genuine that to sustain anger or irritation would have been like smacking down a small child who cuddled up to whisper, "Sorry," after some minor misdemeanor. Anyway, in the next bed I had Karl Cannon, American, and a good comrade indeed with just the right degree of understanding and tolerance to give me a sharp rebuke when needed.

News of the war was sparse. For some reason newspapers were rare and, in the "del Vayo," there was no wireless. Even rumours were in short supply, probably because for quite a long time no more British came to my particular Villa.

On 20 February I was again allowed to get up and make my first excursion outside, sitting on a large pillow on the beach for awhile. Of course I enjoyed this little treat but, and it was a big one at the time, like my first outing this resulted in more trouble. At this distance of years I can only say that almost certainly the hospital suffered a serious shortage of skilled medical attendants and doctors. Unarguably they did the best they were capable of and worked themselves almost to a standstill, and I look elsewhere—and nearer home—for those responsible for the tragic shortages of medicines and equipment. But I confess that then I was more than a bit peeved that the dressings would not stay put, resulting time after time in the wounds reopening with consequent extreme discomfort, and this went on for four or five weeks. Eventually, partly from the sheer passage of time without any infection setting in, and partly from my cheating and going along to another villa/hospital and being dressed by an American nurse there, some progress was made. All this time, and for a long while yet, my arm was still in full-length plaster. On the 4th March Cannon and I were moved to another villa, the "Rosa Luxemburg," just along the sea front. There, we both agreed, control, treatment, and immediate surroundings were all much better. Though he continued to beat me regularly at chess.

My mail, nonexistent for some weeks, began to trickle through, together with much-needed Woodbines; cigarettes were even scarcer than news. And this, when it did come, was depressing. On the 24th February the fascists reoccupied Teruel. So, once again, after terrible losses in men and materiel to gain a desired objective, sheer overwhelming force of arms had torn victory from the Republic. At the time I admitted that this was a big shock to me. Then came the inevitable attempt to rationalise: what else should one do?

It is not really all bad, for it is quite true that for two months the fas-
cists put everything they had into the attack, while we seemed to be con-
cerned chiefly with taking full advantage of the terrain, and defending
just fiercely enough to make the fascists use themselves up, even if this
meant, as it has, the subsequent loss of the town.

Not very convincing but it helped. I am sure that very few at that time
even guessed at the tragic consequences of the effects of our own dreadful
losses.

Other news followed. We learnt of Foreign Secretary Anthony Eden's
resignation over a proposed Chamberlain loan to Mussolini. Then:

10th March. Much talk of a big fascist push on the Aragon Front.[36] *It*
is becoming more and more obvious that these next few months will be
the critical and decisive period for Spain. The London Non-Intervention
Committee apparently still talking about the withdrawal of volunteers.
No confirmation yet of a talked-of General Election in England.
Chamberlain seems to have made the loan to Italy and got away with it.
Cigarette issue to-day, first for sixteen days.

11th March. The fascist drive appears to be continuing. There is a
rumour that the famous "Campesino" is bringing a sabotage charge
against our Air Force.[37] *I can't see that. It is true, of course, as we are*
always being told, that ours is much smaller than theirs. Their planes
simply come over and bomb at will, time after time, all day long. Ours
are presumably doing the same—but some place else. Nothing is more
heartening than to see your own planes come over and give them a taste
of what they are giving you, but this very seldom happens.

When I could move about a bit I used to go to the one-time salon of this
house and listen to the wireless. So we heard of Hitler's putsch in Austria,
the arrest of the Austrian Chancellor Schuznigg, and of Chamberlain's—

Given way completely to the fascist demands, made a loan to Italy
and is now negotiating the recognition of Franco, and Italy's conquest of
Abyssinia, as well as granting a free hand in Austria and Spain.

Franco's drive went on.

At a meeting to-day (14th March) there was an appeal to all those able to go back to the Front.

In the following days I reported sadly on the capture of Alcorisa by Franco's troops.

It is tragic for war to come there, where we spent our Christmas; where I had a coat repaired and they would take nothing for doing it; where everything seemed so peaceful.

About this time I had a very welcome visit from Arthur Nicoll and Jimmy Arthur of the Anti-tank Battery. They were on their way to Valencia to get one of the guns repaired.

According to them the recent fighting was a rout, not a retreat. They say they lost one gun and both the others are out of action. Willoughby was killed, and several others wounded, including Otto Estenson again.

The fascist attack eased off temporarily, as it very soon transpired.

22nd March. No fags for twelve days. Praying for mail and got one—a pamphlet by Harry Pollitt!

Great news if true—France has reopened its borders to allow arms to come through![38]
Then, with one hour notice, a large number of us were sent south a hundred and fifty miles or so to Murcia. We went on a well equipped and comfortable hospital train.

24th March. Taken to station at 6.30 P.M.. Train came in at 8.30. Started at 11 P.M. As a walking case I am in an ordinary compartment, but this is the finest train I have yet seen in Spain, previously used on the Alicante-Madrid-Saragossa route. About 11.30 they took us along to the restaurant car and fed us; quite good.

25th March. Slept fairly well and got coffee and bread about 9 A.M. Passed through Valencia during the night. They appear to be taking us to Albacete first. Very enjoyable trip through some excellent country.

Later. Reached Chinchilla, famous for its rabbits and a very pretty place, about mid-day. Here, those who are going to Albacete left us and

we went on South-Eastwards towards Murcia. They fed us soon after-
wards. To my regret, Karl Cannon left us for Albacete.

This is very grand and mountainous country, with what seems to be a
greater degree of prosperity about the fields and villages.

Arrived at Murcia about 5 P.M. Taken to the Casa Roja Hospital, a
very grand affair. It has five floors and all "mod-cons." I'm told it was
previously a quite smart hotel.

However, and not surprisingly, the mod-cons did not extend to a working lift. As we were unloaded from the trucks and coaches which had
brought us from the station, each "walker" was given a card showing floor
and room number and told to start climbing. Mine was right at the top.
Stretcher cases were to be carried up, mostly by young Spanish girls. An
officious male orderly, seeing my cane and limp, brusquely ordered two
pretty chicas to put me on a stretcher and carry me. I managed to decline,
and joined the slow and rather painful climb floor by floor. As our decreas-
ing numbers reached the third and then the fourth floor, the poor young
stretcher bearers were forced to rest their burdens every few paces. I was
stopping frequently myself and on a half-landing between the fourth and
fifth floors paused as one such party struggled into view. The passenger
was a lively young Spaniard. He was sitting on the stretcher with a lightly
bandaged leg hanging over each side and indulging his very personal sense
of humour by noises and gestures roughly translating as—"Gee up! Whoa
there! Gee up!" all of which his two almost exhausted carriers took in
extremely good part. Then, with the final landing only a few paces away,
sirens wailed an air-raid warning. Like a flash the patient was off the
stretcher and bounding down the stairs. Looking over the well we saw
him still making good time right to ground level. To their everlasting glory
those two girls just sat on the stairs and laughed and laughed. I joined
them.

My first favorable impression of Murcia was not belied by better
acquaintance, of either hospital or town. One of the doctors working on
my floor was the young German who had crossed with us from Sete, in
France. His English was good and we exchanged brief notes on our experiences since then.

I soon found my way to the roof of the Casa Roja, which gave a beautiful as well as interesting panorama, overlooking much of the town, with
mountains providing an impressive backcloth. Nearby I saw a very impos-
ing church.

It is more than twice the height of this place. I should love to go up to the top. On this side of the town I can see at least a dozen others, some of them seemingly Moorish in origin, with turrets and painted cupolas. It is like another small world up here, for all around are people out on their flat roof-tops, living, working, eating and sleeping.

In my subsequent wanderings I found the church. There was no chance of getting in, for the place was securely locked. However, there was much to admire from the outside, and to my pleasure I saw no sign of deliberate damage—indeed, many of the lower windows were protected by thick boards and sandbags. Then, on a large notice board fixed to the massive front doors I read what I shall never forget:

Comrades! Respect the labor of your Companions of Yesterday.

Murcia was quite a lively town. It even had a black-market restaurant which, I confess, I went to more than once. Soon after arriving I received about half the back pay due to me; two or three meals accounted for most of that, however.

One day I was sent to the University Hospital for more x-rays on my wrist. There I met Ramón, the orderly from Huete. He told me that Huete Hospital was no more, the staff dispersed, he himself being sent here. He did not know the whereabouts of Renee or Isabel. His brother, a captain in the Republican Army, whom he had so proudly taken around the wards during my visit there, had been captured during the recent Aragon fighting. "So he is dead," he said, simply. I was sad for him. And then, to my added distress, he told me of Anita's death in childbirth. We said goodbye with a silent handshake and embrace. His news of that dear person, Anita, upset and depressed me.

But another reminder of Huete Hospital was to come. Somewhere in the maze of corridors of that large building I saw none other than Sam Parkes—Sam the unforgettable. He bore down on me, rather than approached me. I swear he still wore the same pyjamas he had worn the last time I saw him, still the same sloppy slippers; his hair was awry and he was unshaven. His loose grin was there as before and, poor chap, so too was that outstretched arm in its cradle. It was no better. "I've got all the medicos foxed," he said proudly. "They don't know what to do next—I've beaten them!" But the persistence of his wound over so many months was taking its toll on his general health and his spirits. He still managed a brief flash of his previously infuriating "brightness," but he could not keep it up. Life had clouted him too hard and too often. In the half hour we spent together he did not once mention the word "adventure." He told me, soberly, "They say that if they take the arm out of its cradle it will all open up again, and if they don't they're afraid I'll lose the use of my arm completely." But then he added, "I think they are going to send me home to England soon." I never met or heard of him again. I think it probable that he was sent home and can only hope that better treatment and care did in fact manage to save something for him of his quest for adventure.

Ominous reports and rumors of renewed fascist advances began again.

3rd April. Murcia is contributing its share of the two divisions of youth which are being called for. And by gosh some of them are young. Obviously things are very serious.

Should they get through to the coast it would, I think, be the beginning of the end of the War, for then Catalonia would be cut off from the rest of Spain.

6th April. The papers announce the formation of a new Government, but details are scarce. It seems that Negrin is still Premier and he has also taken over the Ministry of Defence. But of the general composition of the Government I know nothing.

Nor did I have the slightest idea of just how serious was the crisis of those days, and how nearly Prieto, soon dropped finally by Negrin, came to attempting a negotiated peace in secret talks with Franco's emissaries. By 7 April we learnt that Prieto was out and read with relief of the Government's determination to fight on—"to the final victory."[39]

The next day was one of tension and wild speculations. Franco had already reached the coast. El Campesino had smashed him back beyond Gandesa. The Government had fled to France. Negrin had persuaded France to give the Republic the aid it so desperately needed. Spanish papers confirmed the reopening of the French border and we all, I think, blandly assumed this meant the speedy arrival of guns and planes for the Republic. Meanwhile, Franco's drive continued.

All we knew as fact was that the whole hospital was confined to quarters.

9th April. All day yesterday the whole hospital was kept in—for what reason nobody knew. But at about 9 P.M. came secret (!) orders from Albacete that every single member of the International Brigade in Murcia—soldiers, patients, doctors, nurses—was to be evacuated pronto! Two trains were provided and we left about 2 A.M.

No hospital train this. Just an ordinary goods train, like those we go to the Front in, with everybody, walking and stretcher cases sleeping in box-cars, with mattresses for the lucky, or more deserving, few. This morning they gave us, of all things, a tin of condensed milk each. Heading North.

10th April. Making very slow progress. At midday we are only a few miles north of Benicasim. Apparently the bottleneck at the spearhead of the fascist cross-country drive is much narrower than I thought, for the Spaniards all agree that they (the fascists) have reached Mora Nueva, which is no more than 20 kilometres from the coast. So—it really seems to me that they are getting us north into Catalonia before it is too late. This is as serious as it sounds. Only I should have thought that if they do fear Franco will reach the coast, they would not bother about such a comparatively small matter as getting a few hundred Internationals, many wounded, anyway, into a favourable position for evacuation; for I believe that then the War would be lost. I'm damned if I could see how we could hold out for long. Of course, it may be that they are bringing us nearer the Front to speed things up for our eventual return to Brigade.

We have now been in this spot for some hours. It was heavily bombed last night and so, apparently, was another place ahead, Tortosa, and we are waiting for the line to be cleared.

11th April. We stayed at the last village, Mianes, until about 5.30 and certainly however near or far the Front is we could hear the guns quite distinctly. Every minute Tortosa and the danger ahead assumed greater proportions. Station chiefs, Military and Medical Brass-hats anxiously conferred on the chances of our getting by. Finally we crawled into Tortosa over the all-important railway bridge, which had been hit but not fatally. Tortosa certainly was in a mess. Except for villages right in the Front line this was the worst I have seen. Curtains fluttering bravely from what had once been windows for some reason stick in my mind.

Anyway, the bridge held for our crossing. No enemy planes appeared during the hour taken by the operation; once we stopped for fifteen minutes right in the middle! Heavy shell fire grew appreciably nearer and louder, but it was bombing we feared most just then. When at last the train creaked and jerked its way forward, the collective sigh of relief from the hundreds of us on board must have been audible for miles. Safely over, and now past the spearhead of Franco's advance, the train put on more speed and we went on toward Barcelona.

In our comfortless box car we sat silent and subdued. Our relief was tinged now with other emotions. Every added mile diminished the danger to us personally, but in the sinister threat of Franco's advance to the coast and the consequent splitting of the Republic, we saw a greater, tragic danger to Spain and all we were fighting for.

In the stories I was later told of that devastating fascist breakthrough of April-May 1938, the name of Belchite featured prominently. The 15th Brigade, the British Battalion and the Anti-tank Battery fought and suffered much in and around that small town.

It was there, on a bright warm day in May 1981 that our coach took us. We had driven through the bustling town of Tortosa and up into the Aragon hills. I saw that bridge again, with a train speeding unconcerned across it. Soon came names of places readily recalled—Calaceite, Gandesa—then we were there.

For all of us, Belchite was a shock. As we clambered from the coach we saw a ruined town smashed and shattered by bombs and shells, every house and building little more than crumbling brickwork, bits of staircases still hanging crazily in space, a rusting bedstead defying gravity as it clung to a few feet of upper flooring. The once neat streets were heaps of rubble, the Square desolate, no meeting place now for any other than the dead. Outstanding, even in its destruction, was the church; roofless, an empty shell, it still kept its tower above the battered walls. The Church yet had its eye on its people.

We scrambled through and over these ruins of Belchite, deliberately left as it was when the last shells and bombs smashed into it. Had Franco ordered this to bring home the horror and bestiality of war—all war—he might have gone a little way toward deserving the title of "Gallant Christian Gentleman" bestowed upon him by a once prominent English politician. However, his point plainly was the horrors of war inflicted by "reds": a memorial to "Our Heroes" erected by the Phalange drives this lesson home.

Here in the ruins you can still pick up, if you look hard enough, pieces of shrapnel, a scrap of crockery, a twisted spoon. Hughie Smith, another of our Anti-tank Battery, afforded us some welcome light relief by calling for volunteers to look for a tin box he had been compelled to jettison "the last time I was here," in the undignified hasty retreat. "I had the Battery's records *and* their pay in that box," he said, with renewed as remembered anguish, "and I just had to dump it somewhere, somewhere around here," and he waved an expressive arm at the ruins. We were grateful for the easing of tension.

As always, the BBC television people were busy here. Hardened as they were to tragedy and pathos in other parts of the world, they were not unaffected as they trailed us through this desolation.[40]

In some respects, our fast-moving itinerary was a help. It meant we had little time to indulge in our bitter-sweet memories, though every man and woman of our tour party left Belchite and all that it reminded us of with more than a touch of sadness that day. But the coach was ready to leave and soon even the ruined church tower was out of sight. We were a subdued party; the pages of history are not so lightly turned back.

My diary still had a lot to record about that unforgettable train ride up from Murcia in the South to Catalonia.

> *11th April. Later. We made Barcelona some time during the night and at 10 A.M. are still here. Things are being sorted out a bit. It seems to me that nothing like this has been attempted before. We are not allowed out of the station but even from here Barcelona looks badly shattered and disillusioned and interested more than when I was here before. Of course, I should like to get out and see what the town really looks like. Haven't seen a paper for some days, but by God the narrowness of that bottleneck is a damned unpleasant surprise to me. Why, why, why doesn't France send in the guns and so forth said to be waiting at the border before it's too late?*

That was not the only unpleasantness. Security never was outstandingly successful in our experience and, although we were not allowed to leave the station—officially we were even supposed to stay in the cars—little or nothing was done to prevent others from getting to us. During the morning odds and ends of Internationals, the inevitable drop outs, inescapable in any army, came around scrounging anything they could get, alternately whining about their ill-luck, or embarrassing everybody with loud and foul expressions of envy of us who—"would soon get a chance to f—— all fascists and shoot some of the bastards like I would if only I could—." But far more disturbing and certainly far more distressing were the many women and children who besieged us almost as soon as the train stopped, begging food, for themselves, for their children, for the tiny babies in their arms. And how desperately they seemed to need it.

Now and then, by some odd quirk in my make-up, I would be too embarrassed, occasionally too ashamed, to express my emotions in words even to my "secret" diary. I could not, at that time, do more than note the presence and purpose of these poor, pathetic people. But nothing will ever erase the memory, and even now I feel something of the shame I felt then as they thanked us, their smiles and gentle words adding to the torment of our emotions. Most of us were glad that we had not consumed our tins of condensed milk. We gave what we had, and turned away as a mother put her fingers into a tin and crammed the thick, gooey stuff into her baby's mouth.

Not for the first time a dreadful heresy came into my mind: was I *sure* it was right to be there, helping to keep the fight going and so contributing to such scenes? But my doubts, like my recently expressed fear of eventual defeat, were kept very private, a thing between my diary and me. Anyway, my moods changed frequently and drastically, influenced very much by the turn of events and by those around me—and lengthy stays in hospital weren't noted for encouraging revolutionary zeal.

At Barcelona all the more seriously wounded were taken off and put into ambulances. Those of us remaining stayed in our now dirty and smelly boxcars as the train continued North. But not for long. At Mataró about twenty kilometres north of Barcelona, we were at our journey's end.

Once again it was a case of best foot forward and follow the leader for all except a few. Within minutes a long, long line of men in varying degrees of capability began struggling through the town, some with crutches or sticks, some with arm injuries, a few with both. I still had my arm in plaster and the long train ride had not done much for the "entry and exit" holes in my buttocks! Soon, a friendly banter was being exchanged between the three hundred or so of us and the sympathetic but understandably amused bystanders. Many men wore just their hospital issue pyjamas, helped out now and then by a blanket or the ubiquitous capote, a shapeless, unflattering cape of coarse khaki. Most of us wore various items of official issue we still clung to, supplemented by whatever civilian apparel we had bought or scrounged over many months. Rope-soled canvas shoes were common to almost all. We could have given little encouragement to even the most sanguine onlooker.

It was a longish walk, I remember. Inevitably the streets soon began to climb up from the town center, and then we saw the huge, church-like building towering above us and the whole town. This was our hospital.

We came to an absolutely newly-established hospital. It is a comparatively new building, of tremendous size and, once again, I think, it was something in the church line, but it is bigger even than the hospital at Huete or Murcia.

There are very few beds here, almost 90% of us sleeping on mattresses on the floor. Only one washing place is ready so far—you line up for it. You also line up for food, which at present takes about 30 minutes sitting-down time for two not very good dishes. If you are on second or third sitting, you might be unlucky. Nurses are here in plenty, but they seem to be short of general help.

The only illumination used so far are candles and oil lamps although elaborate fittings hang from the ceilings. At about ten o'clock last night an attendant came into the huge room—ward—and pulled a few switches, and all the lights blazed out! I wonder if it's just because he was the first to think of trying them? Anyway, he got scared and turned them all off again.

Of course, and not for the first time, I did Authority an injustice. Mataró is right on the coast and the vast hospital (previously a monastery I was later told) was clearly visible from the sea, so to advertise its presence would have been foolish indeed.

As soon as was practicable I was out exploring Mataró. I liked what I saw, but at a cost.

Two meals, evening and mid-day, cost 60 pesetas each. Have managed to spend 250 pesetas in three days, twenty five days' pay! Getting hard up again.

Yet I had some cause for celebrating; they took the plaster off my arm at last. I felt almost lost without it. They said it should have come off two weeks previously.

14th April. No further news except of heavy losses in the British Battalion and the 15th Brigade.

16th April. Walked to a pretty little village called Argentona. Only about three kilometres from Mataró, but they won't take the local money—they have their own too. Having new language difficulties here for they all speak Catalan, which varies considerably from Castellan.

I still keep a 25 centimos "docket" given me as change in an Argentona cafe. We didn't get there in our 1981 tour or I might have tried to exchange it!

17th April. Confirmation of grim fact that Franco has reached the coast at Benicarló, and Spanish papers at last admit it. However, nobody here seems to regard it as the shattering event that I do, so perhaps I'm wrong. But for nearly two years now Republican territory has been lost steadily and now it's cut in two.

Harry Pollitt, General Secretary of the British Communist Party, was here to-day. He said it's not too serious; some form of contact between the two halves is still possible. I can see that, but not to the extent of being able to send or receive aid when needed.

19th April. Bill Rust [later editor of the Daily Worker*] arrived. Hopes to come again soon and give us a talk. Says Wally Tapsell, British Battalion Commissar, captured, and Robert Merriman, Brigade Chief of Staff, killed or captured. Arthur Nicoll is confirmed as Anti-tank Battery Commander—but there is no Battery! One gun was lost during the retreat and the other two went into dock for repairs and were swiped by another Brigade. So, until they get more guns they are now a Machine-gun Company. I do hope they get some more guns soon . . . .*[41]

Accounts differ as to just what did happen to the Battery's three guns: some men swear they were all got out and away in good order. I, obviously, don't know. but about this time saw the end of the British Anti-tank Battery as I had known it.

21st April. The papers report an attempted fascist drive along the French border, clearly with the intention of cutting off what little help we are getting through France. I must confess to feeling rather pessimistic as to our chances now. I have thought for a long time that at its present strength of armaments the Government could not stand up to any large increase of arms for Franco by Italy and Germany. Our capture of Teruel was the signal for Hitler particularly to send extra help to Franco, and subsequent events have proved me right. How the hell to persuade the bloody fool Labour Party at home that it isn't all just a game? I read to-day in a Spanish paper that the British I.L.P. has decided to approach the Labour Party for a United Front—minus the Communist Party![42]

25th April—an entry of which I am very fond—told I must get my backside in the sun to help heal the wounds. Ways and means not suggested.

26th April. A somewhat more optimistic mood seems to be prevailing, but the fascists now hold a stretch of coast for about twenty miles.

May Day, and one year to-day since I left England for Spain. Local lads and lassies came to the hospital and gave us a cheery concert of songs and dancing.

4th May. I shall be glad to leave here—have had enough. It's a nice town but, as I have found before, hanging around hospitals is pretty deadening.

It seems that when I do get back I am definitely booked for the Machine-gun Company of the British Battalion. Well, that will mean new experiences.

10th May. Watching half a dozen badly wounded British leave for home has made me homesick!

It seems that maybe I was wrong in saying that now the fascists must win, although I am by no means sure. Certainly I can see that I was wrong in assuming that the cutting in half of the country meant the rapid collapse of the Government. For one thing, I underestimated the powers of resistance of the Spanish people, but I still cannot see how they can keep going for very long without a great increase in outside help. The next big offensive will show how things are with us.

On 11th May I was at last officially declared fit. But getting away was another matter. A Medical Commission was expected in a week or two for such as me. However, a chat with the Hospital Political Commissar

resulted in my being given the necessary permission and essential documents to make my own way to Barcelona and there—"someone will know
the whereabouts of the 15th Brigade." The thought of a day or so in
Barcelona was very pleasant even though I cursed myself for having spent
almost all my cash. Wisely, I waited until after mid day meal time and then
quite easily got a lift into Barcelona. It was a matter of minutes to collect
my few belongings which went into a small haversack I had acquired
somewhere. My diaries, as always, I stowed in my pockets.

*Barcelona. It is almost a year ago to the day that I last walked
around here. Then, my world was young and contained merely threats
of horrors to come without, for me, the reality. Many signs about of
recent bombings, but still things outwardly are more or less the same.
Cinemas are open, people stroll along the Ramblas and children play in
the streets. It is very good being in a large town again, but I wish I had
had the sense to save some money.*

I took my time in finding the administrative offices I was bound for. The
unexpected opportunity to see a little of this city, now the seat of the
Republican Government, was too good to miss. I walked about its wide
streets, sat in the Plaza de Catalunya, and everywhere instinctively compared what I saw with Madrid. I saw little evidence of urgency, awareness
of the critical issues soon to be resolved, apart from an abundance of
posters calling for "Resistance to Fascism." Restaurants were well filled
with soldiers and civilians. In my assorted, ill-fitting clothes, hardly rating
as a uniform, I looked and felt a positive scruff compared with the many
well turned out young soldiers I saw on the streets. The girls they walked
with arm in arm were as smart as they. A little depressed, I made my way
in the late afternoon to report.

I can't remember that they were overjoyed to see me. In fact, the
office was just about to close for the day. Nobody was there to make any
great decisions such as my case apparently called for. Eventually a
sergeant, an English-speaking Cuban, gave me a letter for a nearby barracks which would take me in for the night. I was to return next day at
12 o'clock. Very tired and aching now I set out to find the promised
accommodation. After a lot of walking and asking directions (and,
largely, failing to understand the Catalan replies) I had a remarkable
stroke of luck. I entered a building which, in the near dark, I thought
might be the barracks, and found myself in a hospital. The people there,

Spaniards all, must have been among the most compassionate and under-standing in all Barcelona. I don't think they grasped much of what I told them in my best Spanish, but I understood them very well. For they took me at once into a large room where thirty or so Spanish soldiers were eating, sat me down and gave me the best meal I had had for months out-side black-market restaurants! Later I was given a bed in a small ward and slept soundly. Next morning came coffee and bread. I did the best I could to thank them and left.

It was still only 9 o'clock. One of my roommates, who had told me he was for some time with the International Brigade, had also mentioned that Barcelona's trams were free to all troops. I boarded the first that came along. We left the plusher parts of the city and I looked out at streets and houses more like those of my native Hackney; workers' homes, and working people, men, women, and children no longer smartly or expensively dressed, nor with the ready gaiety and ease of mind which seemed to predominate in the city's West End. I felt more at home with them, my dress matched theirs. Suddenly, as the tram clanked along, the blare of a siren was clearly audible. At once the tram stopped; driver, conductor and everyone else left the vehicle and made for cover. I stood on the pavement. Nothing happened, so I walked on. Evidence of bombing was much more frequent in this area. Again I looked at ruined houses and flattened buildings: a school, with one end of the low building shattered while at the other end glass windows were still intact. Elsewhere, the usual crazy feats of balancing achieved by pieces of furni-ture, walls, and roofs.

I still had a few pesetas and went into a cafe, of the type we used to call a coffee-shop. But as I was sipping my vermouth—the only drink available—there came the shattering, frightful sounds of bombs falling, six in rapid succession. I remember thinking how unpleasant it was to be caught in a town during an air raid, and wishing I was out in the open.

In the street people were getting up from where they had flung them-selves and in a minute or two were again going about their business. No one nearby was hurt, for the bombs had dropped elsewhere, down by the docks area.

It was time to find my way back to my Cuban sergeant. He was waiting for me. He told me that all Internationals returning to their units were to go through the base at Badelona, a suburb just north of Barcelona.

12th May. They told me there was a truck leaving for Badelona, and I should go with it. So here I am at Badelona, about 6 kilometres north of Barcelona. What a hole! It is a sort of clearing house where everybody comes en route back to the Front. Or so they said at Barcelona. It has Madregueras licked hands down. I am in the English-speaking barracks, a filthy bloody place, minus mattresses or blankets, just boards. You expect that at the Front, but surely something better could be organised here. I'm damned if I know how some of these guys can swing the lead just in order to stay in this bleeding place.

13th May. I wonder why they treat chaps who are willing and waiting to go back to the Front so shabbily? Here there are no eating utensils provided, one either buys them or finds an old tin. I, being quite broke, had a spoon bought me by a comrade, and a discarded milk tin given me This is quite large enough to take the twice-daily ration of garbanzas which, with a little bread, is all we get. Plus some lousy black "coffee" in the morning. This is one reason for so many here being completely demoralised. How things have changed since I first came out. Now it seems almost everybody wants to go home. There are many things wrong, of course, and as some of them say, they get "pep-talks" instead of the wrongs righted. Then again, one always hears so much more from the discontented fellows than from the others.

Even though I think much more could and should be done at higher political levels, I also am very definitely of opinion that a great deal of the fault lies with the men. Many of them are bad types who should never have come out here.

Later. Another air-raid, though I do not think they bombed around here, but it seemed that some dropped on Barcelona.

Badelona even then was more of a suburb of Barcelona than a town in its own right. It was a dreary place, a drab industrial area interspersed with rows and streets of poor houses. There was little to recommend it to men with time on their hands, not even if they had money, which few of us did. Two things were in its favor; its nearness to Barcelona, easily reached by tram or even on foot, and a beach of sorts. This latter was small and not over clean, but there beyond was the sea and on decent days we sat there for hours, on occasion even venturing into the not-too-clean water. I met up with Moses, of our Anti-tank Battery, and with one of my old Hackney comrades, Goodman—who actually had some money!

14th May. Goodman said he would treat us to the pictures if we would take him in to Barcelona, he being a novice in Spain. Moses and I obligingly agreed to escort him. What a night!

Went in by tram. Went to a cinema in the Ramblas—not too good. Came out about midnight. Then the fun started. The sirens went off. Immediately there was a rush for the subways. Christ, what a racket from the anti-aircraft guns. They must have at least a dozen batteries. Never having been in an air-raid in a big town, I stayed outside, but all set to dive down at the first bomb. However, they apparently could not get through the ring for no bombs were dropped. After about half an hour the all-clear sounded and we walked to our tram stop. Strangely enough although all lights are now put out at 9 o'clock the trams keep running all night. It is strange, when you think that even in London there is only a skeleton service in peace time too. Of course, when the warning sirens go all power is cut off and then when the raid is over goes back on again. But long before this, sometimes while the anti-aircraft guns are still banging away overhead, cars with their lights on are driving about.

Anyway, we were waiting only a few minutes (with lots of others) when off went the sirens again and everybody ran once more. Then we had another quarter of an hour of antis blazing away, searchlights everywhere and tracer bullets providing the carnival touch. But still they did not get through and the City went back to bed. (It was lousy, seeing them come to the subway in all stages of undress; old men, old women, babies, hysterics, fear). Although some trams were running, ours just did not appear and then for the third bloody time they came over. So we had it all again and still they did not get through. One up for the anti-aircraft. But this time the planes went a long way off, and dropped four bombs. It was obvious from their noise that they were a long way away. All-clear again and still no 71 tram. Then another siren just to make sure everyone had a good night. False alarm this time. Finally our tram came at about 3 A.M. and we arrived in barracks at 4oc. A good time was had by all.

This morning there are the usual rumours of the "terrible damage done in Barcelona last night." One chap reckoned about 500 were killed. So many, without dropping a single bomb. Another went even further and was sure it was German Warships shelling! Well, well. This is a lousy place.

So I had an earlier introduction than most to what was in such a short time to be dreadfully familiar to millions in London and elsewhere.

It was due as much to my desire for self-preservation as to my revolutionary fervor, as much to my need for some self-respect as to my real wish to be once more with the boys, that I tried hard to get back to the Front and away from this horrible Badelona. I had to survive another ten days of the place before this happened. Ten days of anger and frustration.

15th May. The papers report heavy fighting going on at Alfambra and Aliago. This I take to be an attempt by the fascists at broadening their coast strip, thus reducing the danger of any big push of ours cutting right through their pincer.

I have done the kitchen an injustice; it isn't garbanzas twice daily, it's once garbanzas and once lentils.

Lentils or garbanzas (chick peas), the line-up of receptacles—milk tins, jam jars, a tin plate or two, even jugs, chipped and broken—was in place an hour or more before meal times. I have a sketch of these in my diary.

16th May. Definitely cold to-day. Moses and I borrowed 5 pesetas last night and went into Barcelona intending to go to the pictures. Unfortunately there was no power and since it began to rain we came back.

I have never seen such a collection of real, lousy, useless, hopeless bastards as here in my life. The danger is of thinking that they are representative of the whole International Brigade, which they are definitely not. If they were, then I'm quite sure the Spanish Govt would be better off shipping the whole lot home.

It is very annoying when walking around unshaven, in dirty old clothes, and broke, to see, in Barcelona anyway, large numbers of young fellows strolling about in swell civies with their girl friends and to read, after nearly two years of war, notices calling for volunteers. Of course it also adds insult to injury to find them smoking English and American fags—and grumbling because they are not strong enough for their taste!

19th May. Still stalemate on the War Front, apparently. I wish I could find some way of protesting against the sheer bleeding inefficiency with which this whole place (the several different barracks, I mean) is run. There is something seriously wrong. What is most disturbing is that the bad elements in leadership seem to be in control. I believe that Political Commissars in such places as hospitals etc have ceased to justify their existence. I do not mean that P.C.'s are not desirable. I merely say that too many of the samples are of poor material. But then, I suppose that all of this was more or less inevitable for we knew we were not fighting in a Communist army for a Communist revolution. The difficulty is that whereas at the Front there is a great measure of contact and understanding between Commissars, Commanders and men (as a general rule, anyway) here and in similar places one rarely if ever sees the Commissar, and knows the Commander only by seeing his signature over a decree giving guys ten days prison for being drunk or something like.

Went down to the beach and watched the fisherfolk pulling in a net. I wish I could draw to depict the scene. They pull the nets in by man and woman power, and old men, tired out old men and women, even children, took part in the long, hard haul. And when they had got them in, there were just a dozen or so small fish. It must have been heartbreaking.

21st May. I wish it would turn warm and stay that way for a while. This time last year it was scorching hot, but that was in the central areas.

Difficult to judge with any accuracy the feelings and thoughts of the people around here. Unless you really get to know them and to talk with them you cannot expect to understand them. But I am quite sure one thing is true: there is much more distrust, lack of sympathy and enthusiasm here than there is in the Southern half of Spain. What a long way there is to go yet.

(In later weeks and months I had cause to regret this rash generalization.)

23rd May. I've got clear of this place at last! I can go back with the next draft to Brigade. Not today, though, there is no transport.

That same day those of us in the British barracks got some back pay. Moses thought I was mad to be leaving just when we would have some money!

25th May. Well, left this morning at 10oc. They gave us a few fags, the first for ages, and some food and shipped us off.

Later. Made up with the Brigade and as expected drafted into the British Battalion, No. 1 Company, No. 3 Section. This Company has all the ex Anti-tanks in it and my Section is under Otto Estenson. Suits me fine. We are at a little place called Torrega which seems very pretty. I believe we are N. East of Lerida, where there is heavy fighting—we, apparently, are pushing. Sounds of heavy artillery. We are in reserve here, under stand-by orders.

26th May. All out in the open and it was bloody cold last night. Well, my spell in the infantry has been very short! Division has dug up an antiquated anti-tank gun, one only, and eight of us, including George Baker, which is good, are now once again Anti-tanks! Haven't seen the gun yet.

Later. We are moving up, the whole 15th Brigade. We, the Anti-tank Section (!) have been attached for the time being to the Brigade Machine-gun Company. So far, getting out of the infantry has been a help, for we need a truck to transport the gun (it isn't quite small enough to carry, thank God) and so we once again get a lift. Neither do we have rifles to hump around. We have moved up about 20 kilometres towards Lerida but are still well behind the Line. Have found a decent barn to sleep in. So far so good.

27th May. Slept pretty well last night but have not yet found a kitchen which would feed us. Bummed a bit of grub last night, but could not get a (very rare) chocolate and fags ration. Found a cherry tree this morning and fed well off that.

Later. Have had coffee and bread now, 11 A.M., but still can't get our cigarettes. Apparently this Machine-gun Company is being fed by the Transmissions people, and they are to feed us too. They said they had not drawn rations for us but that it will be all right from now on.

We never did catch up on that chocolate ration! Very, very occasionally such treats came our way and we swallowed them gratefully, whether it be a small square of chocolate per man, or a tin of condensed milk to share between half dozen or so. Almost invariably they were sent out by some supportive organization in Britain or America and, despite miniscule quantities and rare appearance, helped to keep alive our recollections of sweets, even though resulting in some strange mixtures going into our stomachs. Huddled in a trench on a winter morning we might breakfast on cold stew and a mouthful of marzipan, washed down by cold ersatz coffee. Impossible to describe the importance such small additions to our diet made. I know we were all angry not to have received this one.

Haven't had much time yet to sort myself out, moving so quickly. However, it's grand to be back with chaps that are not always moaning and grousing and wanting to go home. It is quite true that we are pushing on this Front and everyone feels very optimistic about it. What a change to hear talk like this after Mataró and Badelona!

At the moment we are dissecting the "Baby." It's a shame to have to put up with one little gun like this after the three beauties we had. This one has two high wheels, about three feet six inches diameter, a tiny barrel of three feet long. It fires a midget shell $1^1/_2$" in diameter and six inches or so in length. Rumour has it the shells are pulled back on a string after firing. Still, Hugh Slater, now Chief of Staff to the 15th Brigade, says there is some chance of us getting 3 more real guns in the future.

V

June-August, 1938
The Battle of the Ebro I

Rejoining the Brigade was like waking from a nightmare to find all is well. I felt, thought, and acted like another being from the angry, frustrated chap I was at Badelona. Watching and listening to my comrades of this new set up, I was satisfied. We were a well-matched group, too. Chris Smith and I knew each other well; George Baker, I have written much of already—I was very glad to be with him once more. Ben Glazer, active in London's Unity Theatre before coming to Spain, had his own special entertainment to offer at almost any time, though he was an excitable man liable to blow-up if provoked. Hughie Smith, another Scotsman like Chris, and myself, completed the number of Britons. Then there were our three much-liked Spanish comrades: Montesinos, a young lad from Valencia; Barnardo, not much older though even better looking; and Eduardo, older and quieter than his two compatriots. Yes, we made a good team. Chris, a sergeant, was in charge. Years later I learnt that I had him to thank for my being in the crew at all. Slater, having determined on Chris to be in command of this new found gun, had invited him to pick his team. Thank goodness I returned when I did!

With the sound of artillery varying in volume and direction as we moved from Torrega to Golmez, from there to Mollerusa, and finally to Marsa, near Falset, the next few days were busy ones for the whole of the Brigade. A Republican attack was under way in the region of Lerida and it was to support this that we moved into a more suitable position.

But—

30th May. Official information from Brigade says that since the element of surprise has been lost, our attack has been halted.

Gloriously warm now. Brigade had ordered that all Battalions and other units have 8 hours training a day. But we, with the Machine-gun Company, appear to have been forgotten.

1st June. We are at, or rather just outside, a village called Marsa, which is near Falset, about 15 kilometres west of Reus and roughly the same distance behind the Lerida-Tortosa Front. We are camped in a very pretty valley, with rugged hills and mountains around.

The valley extended for some miles and the whole 15th Brigade was encamped along its length. The Machine-gun Company, with us attached, were nearest the village, about a mile away.

Went into the village for a short while. Apparently nothing in the shops though, oddity of oddities, there was a street peddler from whom we bought shirts, socks, handkerchiefs and underpants! Good. Wasn't able to stay long, so maybe there is more to be seen.

The seven weeks we spent at Marsa were as near to being positively pleasant—allowing for occasional "hiccups"—as, in the circumstances, we dared hope for. There were the usual grumbles about mail, food and cigarettes, the customary alarms and excursions emanating from Brigade and Battalion, some to-be-expected rows, though I cannot recall any among our eight, and, towards the end, boredom and impatience for more positive action. Had we foreseen what was to follow this protracted period of rest and training we would have begrudged the passing of every minute. Meanwhile we—our eight, that is—trained a little, lazed, swam and sunbathed a lot.

4th June. Went out with the gun this afternoon in a feeble effort to convince the Powers that Be that we are in fact training. No news of any sort.

6th June. Took the gun for a short walk this morning. The Battalions were engaged in capturing some surrounding villages in a mock battle. We continue to be forgotten. I wonder when the war is going to start again for us?

7th June. No news of anything. Liar! The Brigade Commander, Copic, is leaving and going to some other Brigade. A Spaniard is taking over from him.[43] Went this evening to see some of the guys in the British Battalion farther along the valley. They are still working hard.

We had found a grand pool for swimming, in a rocky area between us and the village. Secluded, and with plenty of depth of water, it was ideal.

9th June. Shades of Jarama! Went swimming, since it was terrifically hot, but then came rain, heavy rain. It lasted for hours. We took our blankets underneath a little bridge and now have a big fire going, drying out. I spent most of the night playing chess with a Czech of the Machine-gun Company who has made a set out of bread! He is a most industrious guy. From the first day here he smelt rain, so he dug out the biggest stones from under the bridge (luckily for him and us the stream is dried out), carted God knows how many cwts of sand from the bigger stream, just across the road, to make a bottom, gathered reeds and branches for a bed, and now has comfortable and dry sleeping quarters. How many years of soldiering to make me like that? How many wet nights?

No mail yet, no fags. I wish I could get that 50 Cyril and Betty sent me weeks ago!

11th June. When the hell is this war going to kick off again for us? Don't misunderstand me—I'm not exactly anxious for it. Only this hanging around seems strange.

Later. One big laugh. Word came through that the whole Brigade was to be reviewed by Negrin, Premier of Spain. We eight cleaned up a bit, then lined up on the road with the Machine-gun Company. But, as far as we were concerned, the "Review" consisted of four big cars belting through at about 60 mph. The joke was that nobody was sure whether his car had gone through, so we all stayed put saluting any damned car that came along for the next half hour, until a runner came from Brigade to say that we could stop saluting stray cars because Negrin had passed through twenty minutes ago!

Had a letter to-day. I have found an unknown admirer. I keep getting unsigned letters from someone—it reads like a girl—who always enclosed—Party leaflets. "Fight Fascism!" "What are you doing to prevent War?"—and not a single fag!

14th June. Germany's ultimatum to Czechoslovakia expired yester day, but we have no news of the real position. My own belief is that in the circumstances Hitler will not attack yet.

Strain though I might for even a partial recall, I cannot remember how much attention we gave to this piece of international news. In any case, we tended to see all such happenings through what was, perhaps, the wrong end of the telescope: how, if at all, these events were likely to affect our war. And for resolving even this limited issue we were not too well informed. Newspapers, Spanish or British, came to us in a hit or miss way, often none at all for several days. Spanish papers were either the Communist *Mundo Obrero* or the Socialist *El Socialista*, neither noted for objective reporting. Anyway, printed in Spanish they were, regrettably, unintelligible to three quarters of the British. Irregularly we saw the British *Daily Worker*, unavoidably several days old, and sometimes *Reynolds News*, a now defunct Co-Operative Party publication, which, as a Sunday paper, was likely to be even more behind events. Though it was, for us, a "good" paper. Political Commissars abounded, but any light they shed did not reach us. And, anyhow, anything not immediately and obviously affecting our daily lives—bitter cold or searing heat, hunger or thirst, mail and cigarettes—seemed remote and unreal.

So the days passed with, for the most part, highlights and excitements on about the same level as those recorded above. Priorities remained the same. On the 15th the Government admitted the evacuation of the important coastal town of Castellon. Then the 43rd Division, having been forced to retreat earlier into France by the pressure of Franco's drive in the extreme north, was surprisingly allowed back into Republican Spain, and returned with honor and full arms and equipment. It was said that not one man wanted to stay in France or go over to Franco.

Fiesta time approached. The five British in our unit had arrived on the by then quiet Jarama Front on 16 June 1937. So we thought it right that we should mark our one year in the line on that date. Goodness knows what we managed to scrounge to add to our usual fare, but we all sat around a fire swopping stories and singing. Solly Wellman, one-time Commissar of the Mac-Paps and now Commissar of the Machine-gun Company, joined us as did Miles Tomalin and a few others.[44] Our own three Spanish comrades thought the whole thing great fun.

Ours was followed by the Mac-Paps on 1 July, their first birthday.[45] 4 July, of course, saw the Lincoln-Washington Battalion in holiday mood. But in between, on 2 July, a little excitement!

We are the nearest unit to the village, about a mile away. Just before midday a plane sailed over very high and dropped three bombs between us and the village. I think they must have been meant for the road. All waiting now for the fleet to come along and follow up, but so far this is all. Rather disturbed the villagers.

6th July. These are lean times indeed. No mail, no cigarettes for nearly a fortnight, no extras of any kind such as a little bit of chocolate or anything of that sort. And to crown everything the Transmissions kitchen which is feeding the Company and us is turning out really lousy grub. We know that the food they are given is not the best, we also know there is a serious shortage, we know we are better off than most civilians—all we grumble about is the kitchen spoiling, by sheer damned bad cooking, the food they do get. Oh for the old days, when we were a Battery, a unit of our own, and had our own kitchen, and not just a few guys attached to somebody else.

I know that on that occasion I spoke for all.

8th July. Planes came over and bombed in the direction of Falset. Don't know for sure where they hit. The town had not been bombed previously. We were marched down the road this afternoon for a hot shower at the travelling van. We also got some clean clothing as well. My pants are a work of art; how they managed to work all the patches in as they have beats me. Planes came over again and bombed nearby.

10th July. A letter to-day from Jean. She is the second one to be informed by the Dependents Aid Cttee in London that I have again been wounded! Blimey, wasn't twice enough? I am writing and writing, maybe one letter will get through eventually.

15th July. It seems there is a hectic battle taking place on the southern part of the Levante Front—that is, in the other half of Spain—with the fascists slowly, but I am afraid, steadily making small gains. On the map the distance they are from Valencia looks terrifyingly small.

*17th July. What is happening to our mail? No letters, no cigarettes—
and none issued for the last six weeks.*

*Later. Our kitchen has gone mad! To-day begins the three days which
are called the "day of the outbreak of the fascist treachery." July 18th is
official but to-day, two years ago, Franco began the revolt in Morocco,
Spanish Morocco. On the 18th it broke out in Spain proper and on the
19th in Catalonia. Anyway, our kitchen decided to give us a feed to-day
and by gosh it was good—midday, anyway. We had mashed potatoes, a
piece of fried meat (burro) a small piece of fried ham and some salad—
all in one meal! Blimey. The Company, being composed mainly of
Catalans, is having a fiesta on the 19th.*

Next day, the 18th, it was the turn of the British Battalion to honor the
occasion. Various kinds of modest jollities were arranged, with visiting
groups of workers. Party officials and others from Barcelona. On a piece of
level ground near the village we sat and listened to the speakers, then
milled around trying to get through the crowd and so nearer the pretty
young girls among the guests. Then came ghastly tragedy.

*During the afternoon they held a machine-gun competition, to see
which team could get into and out of action quickest, firing off a couple
of rounds in the process. At the finish of one heat bad control allowed
someone—God knows who—to fiddle about, with the result that one
poor bastard got a bullet at point-blank range right through his guts and
another one through an arm and a leg. The first will be dead by now.
Even with doctors on the spot he'd lost far too much blood before they
took him away. What a lousy way to go. Somebody was at fault and in
my opinion it was the first and second in command of the Battalion and
the chap in charge of the gun for the careless way they allowed loaded
machine guns to be handled. But I suppose it's easy to judge. Anyway,
that finished the Fiesta.*

*Two years of resistance. We've lost a hell of a lot, but we haven't by
any means lost all. Whilst I still think that other things being equal the fascists are in a position to gradually beat us down (witness their slow but
sure drive in the South) I am now not so sure that other things will
remain equal. I cannot understand this latest Non-intervention withdrawal move, but it does seem there is some slight chance either of
Germany and Italy removing their men and materials, or else of Spain's*

Spain Base Map

FRANCE

Barcelona

Ebro

Teruel

Madrid
Brunete
Jarama
Huete

Albacete

Murcia

SPAIN

PORTUGAL

Ebro River

Mola
Torre del Espanol
Vinebre
Garcia
Mora la Nueva
Benisanet
Mora de Ebro
Ebro River
Flix
Asco
Miravet
XVIth I.B. Advance - 24 July 1938
Pinell de Bray
Fatarella
S de Caballs
Corbera
Hill 481
XV th
I.B.
Gandesa
S de Pandolls

Center for Cartographic Research and Spatial Analysis
Michigan State University

Brunete

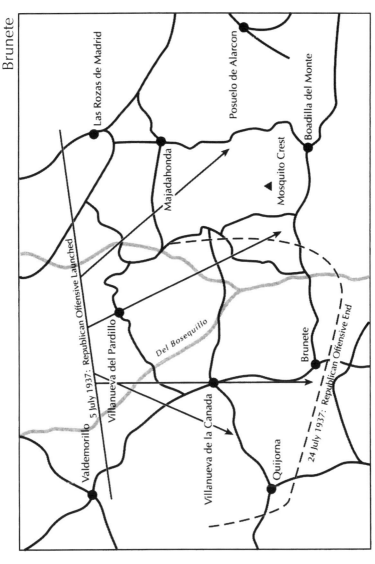

Las Rozas de Madrid

Posuelo de Alarcon

Boadilla del Monte

Majadahonda

Mosquito Crest

5 July 1937: Republican Offensive Launched

Villanueva del Pardillo

Del Bosequillo

Valdemorillo

Villanueva de la Canada

Brunete

Quijorna

24 July 1937: Republican Offensive End

Teruel

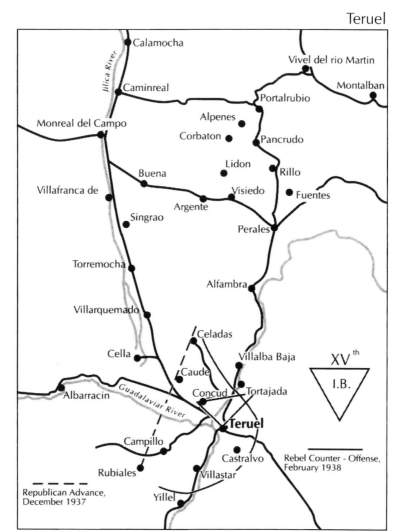

Center for Cartographic Research and Spatial Analysis
Michigan State University

Malcolm Dunbar, first commander of the British Anti-tank Battery. Photograph courtesy of the Marx Memorial Library.

Harry Pollitt, Communist Party of Great Britain. Photograph courtesy of the Marx Memorial Library.

Fred Thomas of the British Anti-tank Battery. Photograph courtesy of Fred
Thomas.

Fred Thomas (left), two Spanish comrades, Saul Wellman (right). Photograph courtesy of Fred Thomas.

The Battery in the field. Photograph courtesy of Fred Thomas.

The British Anti-tank Battery in 1937. Photograph courtesy of the Marx Memorial Library.

The British Anti-tank Battery in 1981.

succeeding in obtaining help itself; in which case as I have said before there will be a different story.

Anyway, here's to the Republic and People, who are able to take it, as these are, and to hand it back. Viva España!

The Machine-gun Company held its Fiesta, though not without some difficulty. Legitimately or otherwise, it failed to obtain anything much to add in the way of extras. Nuts and vino were the only items to supplement the basic kitchen meal—and that had rapidly returned to normal after their over-the-top effort of the 17th.

19th July. The Brigade arranged a Review for all troops at 6oc in the evening. By God it was hot, lined up in the sun, especially after a march of three miles or so to get there.

The Catalan question appears to be coming out strongly in the Brigade. It has by no means been settled in the rest of Catalonia, but I do not think the feeling with which it is being discussed here is typical. For example, a recent speaker from the Commissariat, addressing the Company, remarked quite innocently on "the great fight Catalonia has always waged against oppression." This brought forth much resentment from the non-Catalans in the Company and they refused to listen to his further remarks. Then again, at this Brigade Review, the new Brigade Commander (sorry, I still don't know his name, but he's an Asturian miner, great fighter, captured by fascists, escaped into France, came back into Govt Spain) said, tactlessly, I think, "Comrades, Internationals, Catalans, Spaniards, our struggle is for the freedom, liberty and independence of Catalonia . . . ." This caused more than a slight stir, though I believe that all he meant was that this half of Spain is, in fact, Catalonia.

Even now there are elements in the Government that must be cleared out if Spain is to get the necessary impetus for victory. It was these elements Negrin was referring to when he spoke recently of "those in high position conspiring entirely against the will of the People to intrigue with the enemy. I voice the opinion of our country when I say there will be no compromise—only victory!"

Not long before this, Negrin's great "Thirteen points" program had been the basis for some fairly animated discussion in the various units of the Brigade.[46] My Spanish being by then fairly reasonable, I had been deputed by the Battalion Political Commissar to lead the discussion in our little group. Barnardo and Co. were kind enough to say they understood me quite well . . . .

No use my pretending to recall what we made of Negrin's declaration, but I am sure we found ourselves in complete agreement. It has since been confidently asserted by divers historians that it was also a feeler toward a compromise peace, but it was most certainly not seen as such by us. Negrin's integrity was—I think justifiably—unquestioned.

Next day, with no intuition to guide us, we made the most of the pool on a day hotter than ever.

20 July. We are now getting more or less accustomed to the lack of three things: grub, mail and fags. We hardly take kindly to this, but— well, you know what I mean. No Spanish papers for three days and therefore unable to find out how things are going.

We found out soon enough. The Battle of the River Ebro was about to begin. Within a few days we Internationals would be engaged in our hardest, longest, and last battle of the Spanish War.

From double necessity, to force Franco to end his drive toward Valencia, and to achieve a decisive victory for its own sake, the Republic planned a major offensive, crossing the River Ebro on a wide front and driving forward, it was confidently hoped, to a great defeat of the fascist forces.

Wise in hindsight, the critics explain that in so committing such large numbers of its best troops as well as almost all its precious arms and equipment, the Government sealed its own fate. When, eventually, Franco and his allies amassed sufficient men, guns, and planes to hold and then drive us back once more across the river, too many men, too much irreplaceable material had been lost. Franco, scenting ultimate victory, confidently called upon Hitler and Mussolini to replace his own heavy losses, and soon began his final drive to win victory for fascism and long, dark years for the Spanish people.

But we knew nothing of that, nor feared it when, in the early hours of 21 July we watched the British Battalion march out and, as soon as a truck arrived, followed eagerly. We revelled in the euphoria born of the simple fact that we, the Republic, were going on the offensive once more. Any doubts and fears were easily forgotten—or denied. If we were on the attack again it must mean we possessed all we need for success, otherwise we would not begin it. Therefore we would succeed for, as I've always said, "if only we have the guns and so forth that we need, we'll win!"

This was the spirit prevailing among us all. The truck brought us and our gun to a well-wooded area where we rejoined the Brigade. We sat around in the late afternoon chatting excitedly with men of the British, American, Canadian, and Spanish battalions. In that highly-charged, infectious optimism I found it easy to push away other, more sober considerations of the impending battle. The word came down from Brigade to rest, for that night we were to march twenty kilometers. This time "we" included us eight. Our gun and ammunition would be carried with the Company's equipment; we were to march with the troops. In a dazzling understatement I wrote:

> It will not be so good for us, having to march, as we are used to trucks. [With just a touch of honesty I might have added—And I'm afraid that now we are going to regret the training we didn't do at Marsa.]

However, our newly boosted morale survived the trials of that long night, though sorely tried at times.

> 22nd July. We set off about 10 P.M., carrying blankets etc. Left the road and went off, following a path which soon began to climb steadily and kept on doing so for hours. The path became a track and the track became rougher. My boots, issued to me at Murcia, somewhat tight from the beginning and only rarely worn since, soon began to hurt, a nail in one foot, a blister on the other. Second-hand (or more) when I got them, this was hardly surprising. My blanket choked me, my packstrap cut into my shoulder, the night was stifling hot—in short, I never felt less like a revolutionary in my life. On we went, hour after hour, with a few short stops, obviously climbing one of the lower mountain ranges. Those of the British Battalion, which had left before us, who could not stand the pace sprawled out on either side of the track, deadbeat. The number of times I nearly joined them is beyond count. Dried-up ditches took on the properties of super-special feather beds.
>
> About 4oc in the morning the mountain top was reached and we began to go down. Now we could see the wide valley through which the River Ebro flows, and twinkling lights in fascist territory. An evacuated

village, desolate and shattered on the hilltop, offered little welcome, even failing to provide a drink of water. A weak moon shining right through empty, broken buildings, gave a weird light for the needless procession of tired men trudging the streets. Three lone, die-hard villagers, crouched in a doorway, looking on listlessly. For them, anyway, fascist drive or Govt counter drive were similar things—both meant bombs and shells on their already smashed village; war meant a life in cellars with what they could beg for food.

At last it was light, and we still tramped on, but for me, God knows how. We went down into a valley hidden from the enemy by low hills, and on and on. Until 8oc. Then, blessed be the name of the Lord! We turned into a field, once again meeting our old friend Olive Groves, and it was over. Not 20 but nearly 30 kilometres! We simply fell down and slept.

Later: Everything points to another Brunete. The scorching hot weather, the vast preparations, the short lecture which the Political Commissar has just given us—and the fact that we are promised a tobacco issue for to-night, all these things. The truth is that this is the long-awaited Govt offensive to attempt to relieve some of the pressure on the Valencia sector down South. Of course, everyone hopes that it will also be a concrete drive to get back some of the territory lost in the fascist "Big Push" of April. We are near the village of Torres de España but I am not yet sure of the general geographical position. Bloody hell, I have just managed to get my boots on again! Tobacco issue failed to materialise.

23rd July. Good night's sleep. Lots of men and material moving up all night. Solly Wellman says there are about 130,000 men engaged on a 30 or more kilometre Front. The fascist line here on the river is apparently thinly held and no difficulty is expected in actually crossing. The advance will be in small boats of 5 to 10 men in each. "Last words" from Solly Wellman and the Company Captain. Issue of 2 fags apiece!

July 24th. All night through there was one long roar from the road, with goodness knows how much material and how many men going up, everything, big guns, tanks and all sorts, and men. Seems comic to see little Victoria Park type rowing boats going up on trucks. Wellman says the Front will be much more than 30 kilometres, probably nearer 60. "Gandesa first" is the motto.

Later: Air of expectancy and excitement all around as the night gets nearer. Attack definitely starting to-night or early morning. The 11th and 13th Brigades are crossing in our immediate sector; we, the 15th Brigade, will be held in reserve until we reach Gandesa which our Brigade will attack. At least, that's the idea. Naturally all this happens with other Brigades, Divisions and even Army Corps taking part.

There is a wonderful atmosphere of confidence throughout the whole Brigade. Everybody seems very cheerful. With the beginning of darkness, the road again becomes jammed with men and vehicles. It is very encouraging to see all these tanks and guns and to realise that all this is just a part of the whole. The Company moves out with the Brigade; we are to stay until morning when they will give us a truck. We shall make up with the Brigade again before they cross the river.

25th July. Here we are again, sitting under a tree and watching our big stuff blazing away at the crest the other side of the river.

The Brigade moved out about 1 A.M. We followed on a truck. Every thing seems to be going according to plan. The 11th Brigade have the village of Asco surrounded and are attacking the heights.

Later. They are having something of a show now. They have shelled us a little and are bombing a lot. Planes, of course, we cannot expect to have, but the fascists were able to bring up droves within a few hours.

Later again. The 15th Brigade have now crossed the river, but we still await orders. Some prisoners just came past, and a few civilians being escorted back behind the lines.

Still later. Christ! That last hour had the worst bit of bombing I have ever experienced. At about 5 P.M. we got orders to move down to about 100 yards from the river, in an old, dusty track leading to the pontoon bridge our men have put across. About half an hour after we arrived over came 15 or so bombers and—blimey, I never want bombs closer. Lousy to be once again at the old game of burying your nose in the ground. Lots of prisoners brought across now, all seem pretty cheerful. Avion came over again and again, aiming at the pontoon. Can't see us crossing until they put up another, stronger bridge. They say we are nearly at Gandesa.

26th July. Moved off about 10.30 last night on receiving instructions that the new bridge is ready. Got into the inevitable jam which increased in intensity as we approached the bridge. For hours we hardly

*made 100 yards. Then the confusion was indescribable when it was
learnt that the bridge had broken down.*

Indescribable indeed, and very, very serious in both immediate and
long-term senses. The narrow track was packed solid with vehicles—
trucks carrying urgently needed ammunition and material, others pulling
or towing big guns, many more crowded with men, some light tanks,
everything necessary to the success of the assault and, equally needed,
ambulances to bring back the already many wounded.

For another two hours we all waited, though not patiently or calmly. As
the night wore away with no progress made nor any reliable word filtering
from the bridge, nerves became frayed, tempers gave way. Officers ran up
and down the line of vehicles, waving revolvers and shouting at each
other, more than once coming to blows as each attempted to clear a path
for his own trucks. Now, without any real hope of repairs being completed in time for a crossing, the very real dread of being caught in daylight in this position, sitting ducks for the first fascist planes over, became
uppermost in everyone's mind. And then ensued the nearest thing to a
panic I ever saw. Without orders, or orders from any particular officer
other than the one who started it all, the move to turn and go back began.
Confusion rapidly turned to chaos. No one would give way to allow
another to find room in that narrow track to reverse direction, but that did
not stop several large trucks from trying. At one point it almost looked as
though there would be no alternative to leaving the vehicles and their
invaluable cargoes and making off to safety on foot. Then a mob—there
was no other word for it—of perhaps fifty or so men, following the orders
of an officer who kept his wits, heaved a truck right over off the track.
With his revolver he kept this space clear and began the slow, general
withdrawal.

*So we too finally got back, parking alongside the road under the
usual olive groves, just before the first fascist planes came over. Division
says that things are going well, we have Gandesa surrounded. But the
bridge breaking down is a big handicap, for it means that until they get
the ferry working there is a shortage of ammunition.*

*Some 600 prisoners came back this morning. Some of them are perky
guys, very anxious to convince you that they have really been good anti-
fascists all the time. Only, when they say "Salud, camarada," they raise*

their arms in the fascist salute! I wish to hell we had managed to get across the river.

Midday. We are now well over the river, about six kilometres short of Gandesa. It was a hell of a time getting over on the ferry. They have been bombing hell out of it all the time, and those who were down there working it are bloody heroes. When we reached it they were still sorting out the dead from the living from the last raid. We went inland according to orders. The 15th Brigade is not yet in action, officially, but the British are doing some mopping up. There are some Moors at large, apparently. One Company of the British Battalion has gone out with two armoured cars to deal with them. Hope they don't wander this way in the night!

27th July. I'm afraid we still have not got Gandesa, largely owing to our lack of artillery and tanks. The river crossing is causing a lot of trouble. The Medical Services, too, can't cope with the wounded, due to lack of ambulances. Both ferry and bridge are too often out of action.

Harrowing sights during the night of civilians getting back, some of them wounded. Have not had any grub yet and don't expect any.

Nothing but bloody avion the whole day. Obviously more trouble taking Gandesa than was expected, but the advance along the whole line generally is going well. Vitally urgent that they get another bridge across the river, though. We have few tanks here. Also, food trucks have not been able to get over yet, and we are subsisting on captured carne (meat, in this case, tinned) and marmalade, but without bread, or with a crust dipped in water to soften it, not too good!

28th July. Once again waiting for a truck to take us further up. Or rather, I am waiting, with our ammunition. The others have gone ahead with the gun, trundling it. Gandesa is still holding out. The fascists have more artillery up now, but at present it is concentrating on the front line. Avion has already made many appearances. A steady fight going on ahead and a steady trickle of wounded coming back. Solly Wellman, of the Company, has been wounded in the leg, we hear, but not seriously.

That day was, for me, a very long and unpleasant one indeed, though with a happy ending, I'm pleased to say.

29th July. Well, well. A most exciting time yesterday. Nearly arrested and shot by one of our own side, nearly captured or shot by the fascists, and with-all walking, walking, walking—not with a full kitbag but with three!

Every army has its share of idiots, as well as of idiots who for all sorts of wrong reasons are promoted to officer rank. I sometimes think that perhaps we had more than our share. The one I have particularly in mind was a Czech, as daft as they come. Several times we had seen him ranting and raving about, usually with his revolver pointed at some inoffensive nobody going about his business. He was a lieutenant but what, if any, his specific job was I never found out. Anyway, there I was, waiting for a truck to carry the twenty boxes of shells for our gun and our personal kits. No truck came along. Luckily I stopped a driver whom I knew to be of the British Battalion; he promised that he would be back in ten minutes or so and would then take my load and me. Suddenly along came this bloke who almost went blue about the gills when he spoke of the urgency with which our gun needed its ammunition.

He then plonked a case of ten shells on my shoulder and ordered me to get going. Idiot. I refused. He threatened to have me arrested unless I went immediately. The thing had its humourous side. He was quite prepared to arrest me unless I started hiking ten shells about six kilometres, but would not wait a few minutes more for the truck to come back and take the whole 200. The other 190 could wait presumably. Whilst I was trying to get him to see sense and he was shouting and threatening, back came the British Battalion truck. With the mad Czech looking on (despite the hurry, he didn't offer to help) I loaded the cases of shells. But when I turned to collect our personal gear he really got mad, drew his gun and showed alarming signs of intending to shoot unless I left at once. So I decided that discretion was the better part, etc., and went. The driver was laughing his head off. "All shit and wind, that bloke," he announced. "He likes waving that gun about, it makes him a bit less scared." "He scared me!" I said.

Of course, about two kilometres along, parked by the roadside and peacefully eating bread and sardines, both captured from a nearby deserted house, were the rest of them with the gun. So much for the urgency of the situation. I knew it would be something like that.

But my day was a long way from being over. Chris Smith decided he had better go looking for H.Q. for further orders, the rest of us were to stay where we were. Both artillery and avion right then were relatively quiet, there was shade by the roadside and the bread and sardines not yet all eaten, so . . . . However, what was worrying me was that among our gear left behind were my cherished diaries. I wanted them. I decided to try my luck at keeping out of the lieutenant's way and, I hoped, find our personal belongings where I'd left them. Promising to collect as much as I could I left, confident of returning before Smith.

The first part went well. The lieutenant had taken himself and his revolver to other parts, and our possessions were still intact. I stored my diaries as I usually did, in my pockets. Several small haversacks, tin plates and mugs I draped over my shoulders and around my waist. Then I started on the short hike, glad to have my diaries safe once more, and happily anticipating the grateful thanks I would receive from the others for restoring their valued goods.

But gun and crew had gone. Six hours later I found them again and all was well. In the meantime I had advanced cautiously through recently captured Corbera, climbed several mountains, been providentially restrained just in time from walking straight into fascist fire and the fascists, wandered in the growing dusk over empty fields, passed deserted houses very warily, then up again over another exhausting range of hills each laboriously terraced by generations of farmers adding more precious rows of grapes now left only to ripen and to rot. And all the time the tin plates and mugs with which I was festooned kept up a most unmusical accompaniment to the more ominous crashing of shells and the dry crack of rifles from somewhere now on my left, then, as I skirted a steep climb, to my right, then again as the track straightened, from in front of me. At last I reached the top of one more climb and heard the sweet music of an English voice gently enquiring my intentions:

Where the f—— do you think you're f ——g well going?

My last informant, so many miles back, had been generally correct, allowing for a few deviations: here was the 15th Brigade. In another half hour I was with the gun and the gun crew once more—and the unfeeling bastards guffawed loudly as I dropped to the ground, exhausted but oh, so relieved!

Our gun is now in position with the Lincoln-Washington Battalion. They have had a great deal of fighting up here, and the Machine-gun Company has also taken up positions with them. There was some activity during the night.

We went into action the next morning, in support of yet another attack on the ridge ahead by the Lincolns. The absence of trenches did nothing to minimize the effect of the many trench mortars the fascists have. Gandesa was reported surrounded but still not captured. The Lincolns had already suffered heavily in killed and wounded.

Christ, it's hot up here, weather and all! Could do with a decent meal and some coffee. Have had neither for four days.

But in the middle of an extremely unpleasant night we each got twenty "State Express" cigarettes, courtesy of the Lincoln-Washingtons.

30th July earned for itself nearly four closely written pages. In twenty-odd hours almost everything happened. The crest held by the Lincolns was, to say the least, vulnerable.

The fascists have God knows how many machine-guns trained on it and simply sweep it clean. The Yanks are having a hell of a time, with loads of wounded. In the early hours the 24th Spanish Battalion came up. They said they were going over in half an hour to see if they could take the fascist positions. We stood by to help. Then they went over and immediately began getting it in the neck, poor bastards. With the sun just coming up we opened fire, first making sure our chaps were not there already. The gun is small and inaccurate, but I'd rather the shells did not land near me! The wounded are coming back in a steady stream. With daylight their planes came over, bombing all around us and, for the first time in this action, their big guns favoured us with some close attention, not without success, though not among our gun crew. Confusion spread as machine-gun fire came from our extreme right. They were sighted and we sent over 20 to 30 shells. Then the Lincolns went over yet again in a brave but costly attempt on the ridge. A general melée developed again, in which some said we had not taken the ridge and why did we not fire, and some said for Christ's sake don't fire, our men are there. Hell, what are Commanders for? Anyway, then it all died down and that's how we stand at the moment, with their avion holding the stage and their troops still on the ridge. Altogether, it's a bastard. I would like a drink but there is no water. Although they did get coffee up to us this morning, by mule. First for four days. No hot meal yet, though food is improving. Anyway, I've still 14 fags left!

During the afternoon the Americans made another attempt, just as costly, equally unavailing. Almost immediately after this the fascists staged an attack, but they in turn were driven back, a defeat to which we contributed nearly 100 shells. Brigade had ensured us an adequate supply.

So the bloody day began to end, but not before 18 bombers came over and gave us another reminder of what it's like to have bombs fall really close.

Now, at long last, it's getting dusk, too dark for either avion or close-range artillery, but not quite dark enough for the night-workers in the line to begin. So we get a few minutes peace. Each evening at sunset you can hear the Moors over in their line howling out their bleeding prayers—how good to make them howl for something else! If only we had enough artillery and avion. Dear Chamberlain!

On Brigade orders the Lincolns and ourselves left that position next day, handing over to a Spanish Battalion. We moved over to our left, nearer to Gandesa in the half-circle that was, in fact, the closest that town came to being surrounded. For us it meant a tortuous drive by truck through ruined and burning Corbera, and steep climbs on foot along mountain tracks barely wide enough to take us. I had known more pleasant Bank Holiday Mondays!

In Spanish papers we read of the great success of this battle. Not only were we ourselves making good progress in achieving our objectives, the fascists had been compelled to have their drive on Valencia. We chuckled cynically as we read, too, that the British plan for the withdrawal of volunteers from both sides was "making progress." Also reported was the bombing of three more British ships, making fifty so far. As usual, Chamberlain told the House of Commons that he was sure Franco hadn't meant it.

By 2nd August, which saw us half-in, half-out of position, the too common one of waiting for transport, there was already much to discuss and evaluate, much more to speculate upon. Euphemistically, I referred in my diary to a stalemate having been reached, though I hoped temporarily, on our sector. The truth was, of course, that failure to get arms and material across the river in sufficient quantities early on badly affected our chances of taking Gandesa. Failure in that meant a serious— it became tragic—spoiling of the major objectives of the offensive. We did not then dwell on that particular aspect of the battle. Incontrovertible, however, was the fact of the ghastly losses suffered by the 15th Brigade, British, American, Canadian, and Spanish, in the repeated abortive attacks on Gandesa's defensive positions, Hill 481 above all others.

We had seen for ourselves signs of the panic in which the enemy had retreated under our initial assault. The roadsides were littered with equipment and personal possessions thrown away in the need for speed. Moorish headgear became a popular collectors' item, and even some artillery pieces were left undamaged. At the Flix crossroads a large house had evidently been used as a store and cookhouse. Thousands of cartridges and mortar bombs were found, as well as a great deal of food— including some cases of English Dairymaid tinned milk. No doubt this was all put to good use, but did little to make up for the lack of guns and tanks.

3rd August. As darkness came on the Lincoln Battalion was ordered to prepare to move, and we were told to take our gun down into the valley. So, having climbed up the mountain one night, we climbed down it the next. Only this time we had mules to carry for us.

The Lincolns and the 24th have moved down the road back towards Corbera, not very far. Maybe we shall go over to the other side of Corbera, to where the British and the Mac-Paps are. By the way, I sneaked a little way down the other side of the crest yesterday evening and saw, actually saw, Gandesa.

We have had the inevitable avion for most of the day. There's a rumour that the Brigade is going out for a couple of days rest and reorganisation. All the Battalions have had a bad time. The Lincoln casualties now reach over 200, the 24th about 150, and we heard to-day that the British also have suffered terribly with nearly 250 losses, killed and wounded, so that rest and some reorganisation certainly seem called for.

These bloody planes. We have had so much of it this time, and coming so damned close (the bombs I mean) that I hate the sound of one.

4th August. Moved again. A truck came along about midnight and took us out. The Lincolns followed later. Went through Corbera and are now about two kilometres along the Corbera-Gandesa road. Coming through Corbera in the dark last night was a grim experience, with fires burning unchecked and a dreadful stench. "War the Purifier!"

Could do with one decent night's sleep. However, the night had its bright spot; the food truck on its rounds about 11pm brought, not sardines or bully but a real hot or almost hot meal of stew. It was good. Our first for ten days.

Later. Still here, waiting for dark to follow the Lincolns up into the Line. So much for rest and reorganisation. This is a lousy place to be hanging around in. It's a favourite spot for their bloody shelling. We have been forced to take to dugouts, fortunately here already, probably old fascist ones. Even the local flies are the most vicious ever, and in Spain that's saying something. Had an unexpected good feed to-day. Two of our gang went back on the scrounge into Corbera and got some olive oil from a ruined house (plates and food were still on the table). We then dug up all the potatoes we needed from a nearby field—result, fried chips. They were grand.

Incredibly there are still a few people living in the village. What kind of life must they be having? From some overhead remarks of John Gates, Brigade Political Commissar, it seems that our attack in this sector is finished. I suppose we now wait for their counter-attack. We shall see.

Technically, the fascist counter attack had already started. Aided by our own failure to get vital material across the river soon enough, Franco had quickly brought reinforcements not just of men but of guns of varying calibre, tanks, mortars, and machine guns. His superiority in the air we were already inured to. It is probable that by now the Republican Government and the Army High Command knew that their grand strategy had failed, that once again their hopes of inflicting a major defeat on Franco had been dashed. Short of a miracle, our task now was the all-too-familiar one of fighting to hold on to what we had won. And the high command alone knew at what terrible price this might perhaps be achieved.

Never mind, our morale had a boost when at last some mail got through to us. I collected five letters, with a corresponding improvement in the cigarette situation. Then the rumored rest and reorganization became a reality.

7th August. Last night we had the unpleasant experience of being shelled in the dark. But now, all of the Brigade including us, is scattered in olive groves some few miles back (but still on the same side of the river, of course) on the Mora de Ebro road, south of where we first crossed. I take it we are in reserve here, waiting to see if the fascists begin any sort of counter-attack, or maybe the Govt intends picking another weak spot. Nice and quiet here, not many flies (yet!) and away from bullets and artillery, although their avion has visited us twice already. Some of the boys have gone looking for the British Battalion.

8th August. Made a very welcome break to get a decent night's sleep The British Battalion certainly has had a tough time. About 75% of the old Anti-tank Battery chaps have been wounded and two more killed. Spanish papers report our forces pushing on the Valencia Front.

One serious fault with this place is the complete lack of water, even for drinking. It's several days since we managed to get a wash. However, food is settling down again into a fairly regular supply of two meals a day and coffee night and morning. Also, of course, the grapes are invaluable. Often there are whole fields of them, luscious and ripe right now, deserted perforce by their owners. They make a wonderful meal or dessert. Sometimes I take my ration of bread, squat down in the midst of the bushes and have merely to reach out a hand to pick a bunch here and there. Not infrequently it is the best meal of the day. I imagine they will bring up a water truck pretty soon.

The Brigade stayed there until 15th August. Seven days for those in command to assess the losses and take what steps they could to restore the Battalions to maximum efficiency. Few International replacements were available any longer, almost all were Spanish. It was for all a strange, unreal week, and certainly not without incident. Fascist planes soon found us and helped us keep in touch with what we hoped we had left for a short while.

Then, early this morning, they came over and dropped thousands and thousands of leaflets! They are appealing to the peasants to "come over to our side." This seems to me particularly daft. First, because there can't be many peasants left between the Front Line and the river; secondly, what few there are have been living for three months or so in fascist territory and, thirdly, since Franco himself says, according to Press reports, that we, the Republicans, "were able to make some early, slight advances with the complicity of the peasants," even he can't have much opinion of the "benefits" his rule brings. But I have added a leaflet to my collection.

Ominously, the sound of heavy artillery increased steadily during the week, and soon machine-gun and rifle fire were once more plainly audible. But we remained out of range of the latter and tried hard to ignore the former. The implications of these signs, however, were obvious to all. To general delight our planes put in occasional appearances, once bringing down two enemy bombers.

Great efforts were made by the Commissariat to ensure that food was as good as possible in the circumstances; we remembered we still had to rely upon the incredibly brave chaps down by the river. Subjected to almost constant bombardment they kept makeshift bridges and pontoons going well enough to maintain some sort of supply system for the tens of thousands of us. Some mail came through, as well as for the lucky ones, parcels from home. In our little group we positively flourished, Chris Smith and Ben Glazer both receiving such gifts.

Have just had afternoon tea! Avion staying away long enough for us to take a chance and light a small fire, boil some water and make a real pot of tea with tinned milk and sugar. And we nibbled daintily at cream biscuits.

In the excellent spirit which prevailed among us, parcels for any one meant treats for all. I received almost an abundance of letters and so was able to help out with cigarettes.

What with the parcels and extra effort by the Quartermaster, and grapes, we did well for food. (Though I did report one day on the dire results of eating too many not fully ripe grapes!) Not only did they bring up a water-truck, they went one better.

A really great event last night. We all had, by moonlight, a lovely HOT SHOWER. And were given fresh clean clothes—trousers, shirt, sock and underpants. Oh boy did we feel good! Clean again, if only for a short while. The clothes, though a long way from new, are reasonably whole, not falling apart as most of ours were.

Apart from one or two thunderstorms, which never failed to catch us totally unprepared, the weather continued very very hot. But there was no strenuous work to do and we moved leisurely from shade to shade.

We knew nothing, of course, of the intense political activities involving the Spanish Republican Government and its efforts to achieve some advantage from the inflammatory international situation. It was, remember, just before Munich, and the Spaniards were not the only people who had genuine hopes that the Democracies might be able to curb the Fascist powers, if not by diplomacy then by force of arms. In such circumstances the Negrin Government perhaps saw some slight chance of a reprieve. True, his bargaining strength was being steadily weakened, but he still had some value as a would-be ally in any genuine stand against international fascism. In any case, he probably knew it was his and Spain's only hope now. When Munich followed, Czechoslovakia was not the only country thrown to the wolves.

Completely in the dark on this as on so much more, we were shaken by a rumor which swept through the Brigade like fire.

9th August. There is a very, very strong rumor that foreign leaves are going to be given! That means HOME, for a few days at any rate. But I guess we'll just have to wait and see if there is anything in it.

There was.

11th August. Well, undoubtedly the most important thing to-day is that this leaves business is official! It is necessary to have been in Spain for at least 14 months. As can be imagined, everybody in the Battalions is discussing nothing else. It's great fun now—we five have all filled in our applications; and meanwhile the ruddy fascist avion are bombing and strafing around here like mad! Too bad to get hit now; all applicants about here are digging feverishly, making nice deep holes in which to shelter from all sorts of danger until the Happy Day comes! It's funny, even whilst I was writing that there was the "whoosh" of a bomb coming down and we all nearly went underground by the sheer force of contact with the earth. But it wasn't too near. Although I fulfill the requirements easily, I am not over hopeful. For one thing, they say only 30 are going at any one time from the whole 15th Brigade. The Mac-Paps (Canadian Battalion) are regarding it as official repatriation.

At the same time, all officers of the Brigade have been ordered to buy themselves new uniforms at 500 pesetas each. It's all very strange.

I don't know of any officers obeying that last order. God alone knows where or how they would have got them, anyway.

12th August. To-day is my birthday—cheers, Fred! Twenty seven; I'm getting really old. I can't remember birthdays ever being made much of in the Thomas family, but this one is just about rock-bottom. Last year in Huete Hospital I did at least have a cake!

13th August. This possibility of leave is making me nervous, too. I have just congratulated myself on the fact that this is Saturday *the 13th, not Friday . . . . Really, it is getting us all going, witness the number of times I mention it. There is the simple question "Do you want to go home?" Well, simply from the point of view whether or not I would like to see England, Home and Beauty sort of thing again, then I, like 99% others, would have answered this in the affirmative for the last twelve months. But because we all know very clearly why we are here in Spain, and because for a long time the International Brigade was not merely a valuable but indeed an essential part of the Spanish Army, therefore it was necessary to wait for the time when the I.B., whilst still valuable (as it has proved itself yet again in this battle) was no longer essential, when the People's Army would be strong enough on its own to hold and finally defeat fascism, when we ourselves could say with truth we had served our purpose in helping to build this Army and that now we could honourably expect at any rate a leave Home. That time, I think, has now arrived. One thing we have all wanted and still want is to retain some dignity. That is to say the idea of being packed in bundles and shipped home by the Non-intervention Committee does not appeal to us at all. Now here is an honest and legitimate invitation by the Govt and I for one am being no more than honest in stating my desire to take advantage of it. And that is about the size of things. Clear?*

In the short periods when there is no avion, and when the big guns stop and the sound of the machine-guns does not reach us, it is very peaceful here.

I had no doubt then that very real but totally unexpected possibility of an escape from the War whilst still in the middle of one of its bloodiest battles, carried mixed blessings with it. Unquestionably, there were some brave enough, fired with sufficient revolutionary ardor, to be little affected. Equally I have no doubt at all that the vast majority of us found it impossible to dispel completely the thought that continued survival might mean being among the lucky few—if not of the first batch, then the next, or the next . . . . Meanwhile the War itself again took a hand.

14th August. We are now wondering whether any new attack from either side is developing on this sector, for yesterday and to-day their avion has been devoting a lot of attention to a place which to us seems to be where we left the Line, to the right of Corbera, and their artillery has been slamming around there also. Does this mean a fascist counter-attack, or does the considerable number of tanks and guns of ours which we saw going up last night presage another attack from us? I guess we'll wait and see. It appears that the Gov't attack across the River Segre did not really come off. There has been no further news of it in the Press. But we are still pushing down in the other part of Spain, on the Levante Front, near Valencia, which is good.

15th August. Our little fighter planes are almost making a habit of this intercepting business. They spoiled another enemy raid early this morning, sending 18 bombers scuttling for home in disorder. But they did not come out this afternoon when the fascists had a great time, bombing heavily all round here.

Bulletin on Home Leave! Hear on excellent authority that one of us five will be among the first 8 from Head Quarters lot. It might be any one of us, for Malcolm Dunbar was asked to pick one, since he knew us all well, and he believed our records so similar that he just chose one at random—don't know which one. It seems as though there will be no hitch—except for the fact that there is a War on, and a few other things like that! The Plan *is for 30 to go from the whole 15th Brigade, every six days. That is, six from the British Battalion, six from the Mac-Paps, six from the Lincoln-Washington (American), four from the 24th Battalion (very few Internationals in this) and eight from other units such as ours, Head Quarters Staff, Transport etc. Very strong rumour we move up into the Line again to-night.*

During that night the rumor became reality, the whole Brigade going back into action. He would be a very brave man, or a liar—probably a bit of both—who dares say that leave was forgotten. The simple truth is, I am convinced, that each of us found sufficient reserves of nerve and resolution to push such thoughts into the background. But from that time on it could never be completely forgotten.

16th August. For once they did not forget us, but sent a truck about 11 P.M. The Brigade is now in the Line at Kilometre 5 on the Gandesa-Tortosa road. To get here we had to go through Benicaset, which village surprised me, for it is quite a large place, seemingly very little damage (unlike almost every other village nearby) and with a fair measure of civilians still there. These, under stress of war in general and avion in particular, seem to have turned night into day, for the men were all working in the fields whilst the women cooked or sat at their doors talking and watching the troops go by. I imagine most of their day is spent underground. It was in marked contrast with Miravet, very much knocked about and with only a handful of civilians. This is an area of mountains, cliffs and gorges—very steep ones. The road winds along down in the valley, crushed in on both sides by high and very abrupt cliffs. The Brigade H.Q. is right high up in a cave, an almost impregnable position. The Battalions have gone up by a tiny "all-fours" path, but we have been ordered to wait down in the valley. The usual avion. The noise from 30 or 40 big bombs crashing down in quick succession and echoing around these cliffs is deafening.

17th August. Rotten night. Our own artillery was banging away during the evening, and then after dark theirs opened up and what a din! We got a lot of the rubble landing down here. It seems it is just possible to attack the ill-fated Hill 481 (which the Battalions had slammed at so often from earlier positions) from the rear or near rear. Had cold stew at about 11 oc last night for supper and have had cold coffee and sardines for breakfast at 5 A.M. This is a make-or-break business for one's stomach.

Later. Had I written in this book half an hour ago I should have said, "Very quiet to-day, so far, not even avion troubling us." But they have just been over, 6 of them, and dropped 20 or so bombs as near—blimey, I think they were as near as they could be without actually falling on top of us. I was up by our munitions store, right by the road, and nearly had a heart attack! I am alone. Some time ago we received orders to go another kilometre down the road towards Gandesa, so the rest of them have gone off with the gun and what ammunition they could carry leaving me here to wait for mules to carry the rest.

There goes another bloody bombing party. I imagine they are looking for our heavy artillery which is a little way behind the road. They nearly found Miles Tomalin instead! Two hours of daylight still, and what I am really scared of is an attack starting, in which case our gun will want the ammunition pronto and I have not seen any mules yet. Fortunately rifle and machine-gun fire still sound about the same volume, but 3 of our tanks have just gone up the road.

18th August. Dug-out by the roadside, about 1 $^1/_2$ kilometres farther along the road. Finally made up with the rest last night by waiting for our food truck, at dark, and persuading them to bring the ammo and me along here. No great urgency when I got here. The fascists shelling angle is a bit better here—for the shells. Lots of dug-outs around us, which we have no choice but to use for much of the day. They are the usual sort, about 4 ft in length and two feet high, extremely uncomfortable for the body, but reassuring to the mind. And now, comrades all, here comes their bloody avion on their first visit of the day. Gone right over. I wish the Govt would consider the fly menace. Very hard to find out whether anything big is taking place or going to take place. With the artillery so active and half a dozen or so of our tanks milling about, the general atmosphere indicates something special is likely.

Later. Their artillery is slamming away now and getting right down into this valley. However, I think—and earnestly hope!—that we are safe enough at this precise spot, with the aid of the dug-outs.

19th August. Dug-out, 8 P.M. Whatever the result I try to avoid monotony in these notes, but it is bloody hard to do so when one day differs from the one before only in that it is worse. To-day really has been a bastard. Started off this morning with our narrowest shave yet from avion. We were all in one larger than most dug-out. Miles Tomalin was with us too; he says he is getting persecution mania, he's sure they are following him about. Finding much to our surprise that nobody was hurt we were then able to settle down to 6 or 7 hours steady shelling from their big guns. Ben Glazer is getting very uptight and I confess it has shaken me too. But he won't try to forget it, nor do anything to help take his mind off the effects. Naturally none of us enjoyed it, but it is fatal to let yourself go. The day ended on an avion note.

20th August. I am going to defy the fates by suggesting that perhaps yesterday was the climax of lousyness. True, there was heavy rain this morning (we got very wet) followed by avion, and then a battle during which they shelled us heavily, but so far it has not been as bad as yesterday. But there is still plenty of time.

21st August. I think I'll take back that bit about a climax. Yesterday finished very badly after all. Not only did it start to rain heavily at about 5 P.M., soaking us all pretty thoroughly, but later on our own artillery opened up just as ours and the Lincoln's food trucks came up. This caused the fascists to reply and one shell scored a direct hit on the Lincoln truck. One chap was killed and five wounded. The trucks were just above us, on the road, and where we thought shells could not get. Poor old Lincoln Battalion, wet, and after a lousy day in the Line, got no grub—that went to Hell with the driver. Chris Smith has just been sent for by Brigade, so probably we are to take up another position.

About 7.30 P.M., with George Baker by Brigade H.Q., waiting for the food truck which, after last night's incident, won't come up any higher. Don't blame them.

Later. We are going up the mountain by mule tonight, to the Mac-Paps. Well, we feel things can't be any worse, this spot has given us all the jitters. And anyway, at least we shall be able to feel we are part of the ruddy Brigade again.

This last sentence reflected the frustration we eight felt at the frequent spells of waiting, for either orders or transport to enable us to carry them out. If, as has been suggested, few in High Command knew how best to use the splendid anti-tank guns of our old Battery, even fewer now, at Brigade or Battalion level could fit us in to their schemes either for attack or defense. I see this as an indication of their limited abilities rather than those of our gun and crew. Admittedly of limited range and accuracy the shells could, and did, inflict casualties and damage on the enemy. I am glad to remember that, while it was in our charge, this small gun made a worthy contribution to the general cause.

22nd August. I was reading the other day how a Spanish schoolmaster in Madrid prevented some refugee children suffering continual mental torture from the memories they brought with them from their wrecked homes, by getting them to write freely whatever emotions they felt. The same principle as that which airmen are supposed to put into operation (if still alive and reasonably whole!) after a smash. I've heard they immediately jump into another plane and go up again. Anyway, I'm trying it out right now, for we are having a bloody time. Verily we have jumped out of the frying pan into the jolly old fire. We moved about 1oc in the morning with all our gear, gun and ammo on 4 mules.

Then came the long, long climb up the mountain, behind the Brigade H.Q. We finally got the gun and most of the ammo up on to the crest, held by the 3rd Company of the Mac-Paps, and put it into position. And a most unhealthy position it is too. Not just the spot where our gun is, but the whole damned sector, for the fascists are occupying a hill opposite which is much higher than ours. And so, said he ruefully, we are having a rotten day. They could, if they tried, get us here with their artillery; so far they have only come close enough to make us realise how perfect is the angle they are firing from for them to get much closer! Then, of course, there is the avion. This has been extremely active all day, and from the top of the mountain here we can see them bombing for miles around.

Later—I hope. about 7.30 P.M. I'm afraid it was no use, I just had to quit. We have no real dug-outs here, only shallow holes, the ground is practically all rock, you cannot dig. Over to the right of Corbera, which we can see quite clearly, there has been another fascist attack. For miles around there is a haze from their artillery and avion. Also they have extra large trench-mortars which periodically "swoosh" down. It is bitterly cold up here at night, and even during the day if you are in the shade. Last night, when we at last got down for an hour or two, was the coldest I have been since Teruel. Now I think and hope the day is ended. But—tomorrow and tomorrow and tomorrow . . . . The Spanish papers report the heroic resistance of our troops in the Sierra Pandols (all the ranges around here) and I believe 'em!

A more astute observer might have given more attention to the word "resistance" and its implications.

23rd August. Well, after taking a real hiding yesterday I feel almost perky to-day. Not so surprising, perhaps, for so far to-day has been a big improvement on yesterday. It is now about 8 P.M., soon be dark. But all day there has been a steady battle over the other side of Corbera and a short time ago the heaviest fascist attack of the day was put over, with a tremendous preceding barrage of artillery. Also, here, their artillery opened up and got through the "dip" to land right near us. Then we had another grim circus with 30 of their new, huge, black bombers and goodness knows how many fighters performing all around us, combining with the artillery to throw a haze over the whole valley below. I think it must be the 11th or 13th Brigade over where the battle is going on.

This morning their planes dropped more leaflets, promising "Bread and Pardon," whilst bombing hell out of the villages in our rear at the same time. From the top here we can see back into our own territory for many miles. Range after range of mountains merge at sunset into a dull, flat sameness, but in the morning, at dawn, it is very beautiful. Then the sun rising through a break in the hills catches the River Ebro, plainly seen twisting along down in the valley through the villages of Asco, Mora, Benicaset and Pirelli. Still looking backwards, on our left is Corbera, smouldering steadily but now left alone by avion and artillery which are concentrating their efforts in front of it and to the right. And when the sky is still clear in the morning, looking due north and over the Marsa, Falset area, you can see the snow-caps of the lower Pyranees (sic) which come down nearly as far south as Lerida. But it is only in the morning that you can see these things; and only in that brief period between sunset and dark when, it seems, all men must cease, if only for a short while, this bloody war, that you can be moderately sure of having a chance to record it.

Fortunate indeed that to-day has been better, whatever tomorrow brings, for we are all feeling the effects. Ben Glazer, after a fairly calm couple of days, is again very jittery. He, in my opinion, should be sent back, for he is just incapable of standing up to it all. He has got guts, plenty, but he's sick. Anyway, to hell with it all; it has to end sometime—somehow!

Stop Press: A rumour going around that France, Germany and Czechoslovakia have all mobilised! So far as Germany is concerned, I guess it's no change, but if it's true of the others (and Britain?) then, blimey, anything is possible. Meanwhile it is almost dark and the 'night-watch' has reopened the battle over Corbera say.

The Canadian Mackenzie-Papaneau Battalion, whose No. 3 Company we were now supporting, was still commanded by the same Major Smith who had commanded at Teruel. He had thus defied the fates by surviving so long. By coincidence our own Chris Smith was still our Sergeant in charge of the gun, though, regrettably, the gun was different. We certainly would not have wished any ill-luck on the Major, but it was soon apparent that he and one of his senior lieutenants had no love for us. It seemed they still remembered our refusal to fire at Teruel when we had direct orders from Brigade not to do so. On the night of the 23rd we very foolishly gave the Major a chance to show who was who this time.

Our gun was in position, right in the Line. Our night-time guard arrangements were, admittedly, rather slack. Two would stay in turn by the gun, the rest of us a little way below the crest. But "by the gun" resulted in finding by chance a somewhat better hole a few yards away and, in the dark, not so easily found. When Chris and Barnardo, the first two on duty, were thus tucked in for their spell, along came Frank Rogers, the Battalion's Political Commissar, on a snap tour of inspection of the sector. With him was the Lieutenant who, previously advised by another of their own outfit, zoned straight in on the gun—and found no guard. They claimed afterward that it took five minutes to find Chris. When they did they promptly arrested him! By that time the rest of us were milling around and, extremely depressed, watched Chris being marched off to Major Smith's H.Q., down below a bit. Our crew, less Chris, sat around the gun trying to decide what to do. Just as we agreed to contact the British Battalion (though not with much hope, for Sam Wild, its Commander, was known to be a stickler for discipline) back came Chris—free.[47] Our relief was as great as his own. Briefly we talked things over: we were in the wrong, there was no doubt about that at all, and we could see to it that such laxity did not recur. But we also noted that Chris's release, after a severe wigging from the Major, was an acknowledgement that the whole affair was a put-up job to teach us a lesson. Both the Political Commissar and the lieutenant had gone back with Chris, no one had gone before, yet there was Major Smith waiting for them and aware of the offense. The innocent one was, it seemed, the Political Commissar; to establish this beyond reasonable doubt he later sent us 20 cigarettes! The incident was probably good for us—the cigarettes were, anyway. We were left, though, with a rather nasty taste in our mouths; why try to catch your comrades? In any case, this time there was no argument, we were under the direct orders of the Battalion and Major Smith. Next morning we obeyed with alacrity when they wanted us to fire.

After such a strange night it has been a strange day, rather like "stormy but with bright intervals." During one of the storms a shell landed only a few yards away from our hole down the crest. Not so good. We told ourselves it was a freak, such things do happen. Another bad item was the shooting down in flames of one of our planes this morning by their anti-aircraft guns. A bright spot on the horizon is that we shall probably be moving out in a couple of days. The Big Chiefs of the 43rd (the famous "Lost Brigade" of the Pyrenees) were up looking over the positions to-day.

25th August. Well, the day has not quite yet ended; it is true it has had its very bad spots, one nearly being my last—and even more nearly, George's—for while we were up at the gun a trench-mortar shell landed right on the Parapet—and did not explode! Phew! The last shell last night got four of the Mac-Paps, and another one to-day got another four— wounded, I mean, not killed. We sent over about 40 shells this morning, just after sunrise, and did some good, shifting a machine gun which had been a nuisance to us all. Strangely, it brought no reply until around midday when they gave us a nasty hour or so. It seems odds on our moving to-night.

26th August. Still here, by God. I guess the bloody 43rd must have got lost again.

27th August. I cannot write much of yesterday's and last night's nightmare.

(After which I went on for four pages.)

We have all moved out now and our group is just at the cross-roads of Tortosa-Mora. It is by no means an attractive spot, for their big artillery sometimes gets on to it, and of course avion comes when it likes. But it will have to be bad to beat that last round. We had had quite a good day, in spite of early morning firing on our part, until about 7oc in the evening when Major Smith phoned through for us to fire on a trench-mortar which was giving trouble to the British on hills over to our right and slightly forward. But the sun was right in our eyes as we fired. For the enemy however it was perfect and they let us have it with trench-mortars. It was bad. Then we were told to fire again after sunset; we did, about 30 shells. Of course, this had the same result, though we did have the satisfaction of putting one of theirs out of action; but they must have dozens of them over there. We were lucky, but the Mac-Paps had three more wounded. All this time and no further word of moving out. All we could do was to set our guard as usual. But in the dark it is a thousands times worse, and when they opened up again, landing them all around . . . . Then began a fierce attack on the British lines and soon our sector was brought into it.

Now was the other side of the coin. There is not much worse than being shelled and shot at in the dark. To fire back, to do something, *is a help, but we were strictly ordered not to fire, for some of our chaps were going over.*

I hope I may never have another such hour. The Mac-Paps were at least banging away with rifles and machine-guns, doing *something. George and I both lay silent, both with the same feeling—after all, this was going to be the end. Somehow I was quite sure I would not leave that spot alive. An age later it died down, with us two still living. The British, we later learned, had driven them back, aided by cross-fire from the Mac-Paps.*

Then came one of those happenings of which one dreams: we were moving out! So it ended—for the time being. The mountain track which had been so hard to climb was a pleasant path through meadows going down. At Brigade H.Q. we waited, watching the Battalions filing past, and then got a truck which brought us and dumped us down here. Exactly what we do next nobody seems to know and, of course, we have lost contact with the Kitchen, so have not eaten, but I'm sure I'll survive that.

Never have we all felt an action so much as this last. Never so desperate to leave the Line as now. This, I am sure, applies to the vast majority in the Brigade. The Mac-Paps, the British, the Lincolns, on top of very heavy losses in the first part of the offensive, have again suffered badly this time. Company 3 of the Mac-Paps, with whom we were, out of 92 men at the beginning of the attack (July 25th) had 52 when this action started and 33 when they pulled out last night. In that very last hour trench-mortars got three killed and six wounded. Those mortars have been the chief curse. The British have lost so heavily that they have made four companies into two. Poor old Frank Proctor—an Anti-tank "original"—got a very bad one in the head. They said he may not live. That is a bloody shame.

Later, evening. It has been a beautiful, beautiful day. Already we are conscious of a very definite relaxation of tension, which had reached almost to breaking point. About 4 kilometres behind the Lines, we have listened to shells and mortars falling and have not had to bother about them. Shells have also been whizzing overhead, to our rear, which is no direct worry either. Avion, for some reason, is quiet. We have found the H.Q. food truck and are being fed again. All things are possible and maybe after a few days' real rest in a decent place (I think we move again to-night) who knows, we might be able to stand another basin, even of trench-mortars.

28th August. Moved off quite promptly just before dark last night and are now in olive groves about 3 kilometres from Asco, the village to which we crossed at the beginning of the offensive and the first captured. One thing, we are back with the grapes! But all is not well with the world, for we have just received an order to prepare to move. Just that, nothing more.

Later. Worse and worse. We are all very depressed, for we have been told that we and our gun are being transferred or lent to the 13th (German) Brigade. This is bad, for we do not want to leave our own Brigade, we do not want to go into action again just yet (no human being would) and last but not least if there is anything in this Leave business, that would put the tin hat on it. Not to mention such matters as mucking up our mail and putting us all among German speaking Internationals. Oh blast it!

29th August. Well, well. Things have not turned out so badly after all. The evening brightened considerably for us when we got some mail. I had three letters, the tobacco situation being again miraculously saved. Also, bits of news came to us such as that our 15th Brigade was likely to be going into action again in a couple of days. Hence, we argued, if that is so they will need all they have, including us, for themselves, and won't be lending any out. So we turned in, feeling better.

But around midnight a truck turned into our field and a voice yelled in Spanish—"Where are you, Anti-tanks?"

Oh well, it's come. They gave Smith an order from our own Brigade and—lo! The gun was to go, but not us! They could take the bloody gun and welcome. They did. We were ordered to attach ourselves to the Machine-gun Company (with whom we had been quartered during the Marsa spell) and await further orders. We have also heard talk about there being some real anti-tank guns around somewhere.

So this morning we made it over to the machine-gunners who, by the way, were very pleased to see us, and altogether things could be a lot worse. They and we feed with the British Battalion. I mean, of course, we are all fed by the Battalion, their kitchen truck now including us on its rounds. It will be good if we get a real gun out of all this. In any case, even if they turn us into infantrymen (which would be bad enough!) at least we would stand a chance, whereas we feel that judging by the anxiety of the 13th Brigade chaps to get the gun, life would be one long chance with them—or, alternatively, no chance at all!

Well, Franco has at last published his reply to the Non-intervention Committee's Withdrawal Plan. He says, in effect, that if all steps are taken to ensure that the Republic cannot possibly win, then he is willing to think about it. What a piece of sheer damned impudence.

30th August. We are simply settling down for a rest here, since we have no orders at all. There seems to be no sign of any imminent move, and rumours are again rife. Harry Pollitt has been out and there is talk of the Leaves beginning soon.

Later. They are more than rumours. Leaves are starting right now, and George Baker is the first to go from our group. He deserves it. But we are all het-up now, hoping we all of us get it soon.

George has gone, and we all miss him, I particularly, for he was always a good pal.

That was all the notice George got from me that day. I did indeed miss him.

Since then I have read a great many personal reminiscences of those harrowing days. Not once have I seen a reference to this offer of Home Leave. Why not? I wonder. Is the omission the result of an obligingly faulty memory, or the absurd notion that a good revolutionary is and must be seen to be above such human emotion as fear? George Baker was a very brave man and as dedicated to the Republican cause as any man among us British volunteers—brave enough, quite rightly, not to hesitate to accept this honorable reprieve.

VI

September, 1938
The Battle of the Ebro II

So the First British Anti-tank Battery ceased to exist. Not since the retreats of April had it been a Battery; for even longer it was of Spanish/British composition. We eight, trundling our little gun around, well aware of its limitations and inadequacies, subject to the quips and cracks of our fellows as well as to the varying attitudes of Commanders from Brigade to Company, remembered all too well the respect the Battery and its three deadly guns had rightly earned in past battles. Yet I know we also felt that while we remained a unit, few though we were and with only this humble reminder of our former glory, we kept alive the wonderful, second-to-none spirit which pervaded the whole Battery, from Malcolm Dunbar its first Commander down to every gunner.

Now we were P.B.I. Poor Bloody Infantry, and all aware that the change for us would be considerable.

I had always admitted (to myself!) that we Anti-tanks old and new had undoubted advantages. Of course we sometimes got the sticky end of things, forgotten by Quartermasters and kitchens, now and then endangered as a species by ignorant Commanders of Battalion or Company to whom one or more guns were frequently attached, and many other irritants.

Yet we had been spared much of the foot-slogging, the rifle-humping, the exhausting route marches and other trials of strenuous training undertaken as a matter of course in the Battalions—and had paid for this, when necessity arose. Not for us the "fatigues" and "general duties" supplying guards for this and that. Nor had we been plagued by an overdose of authority from zealous NCOs or politicals. But over and above this, we had been spared the worst any man can face in war—to be called upon time after time to go "over the top" under intense and deadly enemy fire. Though on the morning we joined the Company we

141

kept our talk to generalities, each of us knew that this would be the greatest difference from now on.

31st August. Rumours are rife indeed. The one I like best is that when Pollitt was here two days ago, Brigade called a meeting of all Battalion Commanders and Commissars. The question was discussed—what recommendations should be made to Division re the 15th Brigade? For the Internationals are being steadily wiped out and no more are coming from Britain or America. And it was decided, so says gossip, that the Brigade should be wound up rather than die a lingering death! Pollitt has gone to see Negrin.

Things have been quiet on the Front for two days now, judging by the lack of noise. This is all to the good, for if anything hectic started—a breakthrough for example—they would quite rightly shove the Brigade in again even though it was choc-a-bloc with guys due to go home the next day. This morning we managed to wash and clean our teeth. It was not much, but it was good. All of us of course are once again smothered by lice and fleas. Our clothes are just wrecks. Maybe, one day, we shall be really clean again. At the moment I'm covered with blotches from scratching.

September 1st. Last night, after dark, the Propaganda van came up and gave us a concert. It was good fun sitting outside the dug-outs, in the moonlight, with the hills flinging back the peculiar sounds of those fascinating Flamenco songs. To many Internationals these are just one long wail, but I like them. Sitting there listening I remembered when we were in the trenches at Jarama and I heard for the first time Spanish lads singing such songs and, coming back from the fascist lines, the even more wail-like originals from the Moors. There too the Propaganda van would come at night close behind our lines and send over speeches and songs to the fascists.

Very heavy shelling to-day. We have always regarded any real barrage as a prelude to an attack. If that happens we probably go in again.

I wonder where George is now. The tobacco situation is again acute. All day we waited anxiously for mail. I got a letter, a nice big fat one containing—John Strachey's pamphlet, Why you should be a Socialist! *And nothing more. Leo Ganelling, my friend, curse you for a fat-headed idiot for forwarding such nonsense. It is very cold here at night. I guess Autumn comes earlier up here, although the days are still just as hot. Note: I really should lay off eating so many grapes.*

2nd September. The British got a bath and a change of clothes last night. Hope it is our turn soon. Seems strange that September is already here—strange because the summer heat during the day just goes on and on.

3rd September. Let the blow fall soon or late . . . . Ordered to stand by for a move up. The fascists have taken four hills and are reported as having a mechanised division ready in Gandesa. Leave be damned. Got clean clothes this afternoon and were to have had baths to-night. I guess we'll move up into the Line instead. Bombing like hell at the moment.

4th September. We are still here. No baths. The Battle has been on again to-day and I still think we shall move up to-night. How much better we all felt before hearing anything about Leaves at all!

5th September. Still not moved, any of us. The battle continues to-day. I have just come from a hill top where I watched the shelling. They (the fascists) are knocking hell out of two mountain tops away out in front and to the right. So now here we are with evening coming on and we are all wondering—do we go up again to-night?

6th September. Late evening. Rumours and counter-rumours were plentiful until at midday all doubts were settled by an order to prepare to move instantly. We were rushed out in double quick time. The Battalions were out too as we went through the fields to the road. There, every available truck had been pressed into service. We, the Company, were loaded on and down the road towards the Line we went. This was the Brigade's quickest and most dramatic move in its history. The trucks took us to about 3 kilometres river-side of Corbera (much hated place, whose bloody church spire is again in sight. How I hoped I would never see that again). Here we defiled into the fields, the British Battalion also, and now we have been here for two hours or so.

We are trying to take stock of the position, but information is very scarce and contradictory. One patently obvious fact is that the fascists have advanced, and no small distance at that. They now have hills in dominating positions left and right of Corbera.

And now is the time to write Finis to the honorable if sometimes checkered life of the first British Anti-tank Battery. This fact was marked this evening by us eight being given rifles and told to work with the Machine-gun Company. The other seven are convinced that I'm more danger to them in my new capacity as rifleman than to the fascists!

7th September. Slept where we were last night, and were bloody cold too. Coffee came up before daylight (yes we're back to that) and afterwards, as behooves good infantrymen, we dug holes for ourselves, even me, as shells landed all around last night. Found out how dramatic it was yesterday when, after a fascist breakthrough, the Mac-Paps just won a race with them for a strategic hill.

Later. Our Captain came along about 1oc in great excitement and we moved off again. The British stayed where they were. We were under observation from enemy planes and it was not long before their artillery began getting near the mark. We were going along an almost empty dry river bed and the shells came Smack! Smack! Smack! into the bed and the opposite bank. After a few minor casualties we were ordered to get under the right hand bank and keep down. Then some bright boy investigated a nearby house and found a long, dry tunnel running underneath the building, 60 or 70 yards long, plenty for the whole Company. So they ordered us into it while the shelling continued. At dark, grub came up and then the Captain, who was somewhere in front, sent back orders for the various sections to move up to him, which we did. The Company has now taken up positions on a hill to the left of Corbera, on the right of the Lincolns and on the left of the 24th Battalion. It is a bad position, but then so are they all in this sector, for the fascists now have the highest peaks. I must try to get some sleep, for it is about 4.30 A.M. and I am writing this by candlelight in a dug-out.

9th September. I do not quite know what to say about yesterday, the 8th, for I have really used up all my superlatives already several times over. Heavy stuff was landing all around us a dozen at a time, but it seemed even worse up at the crest where it was just one continual smashing. Chris and I were with the Captain in a little clearing and suddenly it was filled with men from the Company and odds and ends of Lincolns and the 24th. They were in a bad state and had simply run from the hill they were holding leaving it for the fascists to walk on to it. But this was another time when the bloody fascists proved you can have too much of a good thing, for their big guns were still blazing away, making it just as impossible for their troops to occupy the crest as for our own. The Captain of the Company was grand.[48] He stopped the panic in two minutes, found that the rest of the Lincolns had not retreated, and knowing that the fascists could not advance until their own artillery ceased, just said, "We are going back up." About half the Company were still up there somewhere, although they too had left their positions (some had brought their guns out, others had simply left them) but until he knew exactly what the situation was he did not want to risk all his men, so he asked for four volunteers to go with him and find out. One Spanish boy said he would go, Chris Smith made two, and because I could not see anything else for it, I made three. That was the lot. Trying to dodge between barrages, over we went, one at a time, racing from one point to another, the Captain leading. It was a bastard, but we all made it over the worst bit and got to some shelter from a banking. Here we found the rest of the Company. Then, a quick bit of reorganising to get guns back up on the crest of the hill, for the shelling was now easing and this was the time for the fascists to attack. Meanwhile a Company of the Mac-Paps, coming up to reinforce us, staged their own show by sprinting across the valley behind under heavy machine-gunfire coming from our extreme left. They made it too, most of them. Then we went forward, at the double, two at a time, to make the top, and a nasty time we had getting there, for our own tanks, from behind us, began firing into the hill, thinking the fascists had already taken it. But at last we fell into the trench at the top, where we were in time, for the bulk of the enemy were still down in the valley and our machine-guns and rifles changed their minds. For an hour or so afterwards we were shooting at the few who had got nearer and were sheltering where they could. One gave up hope of getting back to his own lines and stood up with his hands above his head and walked slowly up to us. And in that trench, with the shelling finished for that spell, and with the comparative novelty of firing a rifle at blokes, I felt pretty good.

Then the Captain sent some of us with some of the Mac-Paps to hold the left side of the crest until we get some more men up. But whilst getting over there, the shelling began again in earnest. We managed to make it, but then that little bit of trench began to receive the undivided attention of half a dozen fascist tanks. You could not take your nose off the ground. The guys from the Mac-Paps were as miserable as sin.

We won't get out of here alive.

I think everybody else has gone back.

The fascists have got round us—we're cut off.

Take a look over the top, Bill.

You f——g well look!

It lasted a long time, too long, and included a visit from their avion which came over low, strafing the trench time after time.

In a temporary lull Chris and I were taken out and put on to the Company's mortars. They can't know how much I hate them. We dug a hole for it during part of the night (forgot to say we had some grub at last about 11 P.M.) and slept in another hole for a short while. Turned out about dawn, found some coffee, and now, at about 8 A.M., are waiting to see what little tid-bits to-day holds. At least there should be no repetition of yesterday's near panic, for we are now reinforced by a Company of Mac-Paps (half a Company, rather, on this particular sector) and a light machine-gun from the Lincolns.

10th September. Yesterday Chris and I were in separate dug-outs not more than five yards apart and yet could not get together from 1oc until dark. It was the longest and most vicious barrage from tanks, anti-tanks and big guns of the whole offensive. Late in the evening their avion joined in and then they got their trench-mortars going on our crest also, so unless they bring up poison gas we've got the lot! After all of it, there was no attack, though some of their tanks tried to go forward on our left. I am sorry to say that Ben Glazer was badly wounded by shrapnel. Our front-line trench was smashed to hell in places, some of the Lincoln were captured the day before—65 we were told. Our Company came off pretty well with 5 or 6 wounded. Anyway, for all their artillery and avion they seem to have made no further progress for a couple of days.

Already this morning, at 7 A.M., our guns are shoving it over, so no doubt we shall soon be getting it back.

Later. (Not, mark you, that the day is finished, but just to help pass the time!) There was a hectic artillery duel this morning, culminating in an attack over on our left during which we again brought our trench mortars into action. Then their artillery drifted away to our left and right, so we had comparative quiet except when their avion came over. About half an hour ago (I think it is roughly 6.30 P.M. now) their bloody guns gave us another bashing, but right now we are having it all our own way with our avion bombing them for a break and our artillery is sending over a swell barrage too. Who says we've got no artillery or avion? Since the fascists started this last drive I think I've seen more evidence of our planes and big guns than ever before. I wish, though, we could take that hill over on our left, where their machine-guns are that keep us in our bloody dug-outs all day. Chris and I are each in charge of a mortar. The other two of my crew are of course Spanish and don't have much to say, even to each other. All the Company is Spanish with the exception of the Captain, Lt Cooper, and now us three, Chris, Hughie and myself; yesterday we were four and a few days ago five. I enjoy an occasional chat with Chris after an exciting dash of 5 yards or so to his dug-out. Very, very tired, and not much chance of getting a good sleep tonight, either.

11th September. We got some food finally after midnight. But alas, off they went again over to our left and off we went with our mortars. The fascists must have had an unpleasant surprise, for instead of just a few rifles and one light machine-gun, they had to face triple that number, for a Company of the British Battalion had come up to reinforce the Lincolns and ourselves. The poor bloody Lincolns have been catching it badly ever since we moved into this sector. It is no rumour but sober fact that the whole Battalion *now numbers less than 100. And when this campaign began, on July 25th, they were 650 strong. I was speaking to Jerry Cook (he was in Huete with me) who was with the Company that had so many men captured. They were surrounded on three sides and could only run for it. He says that 14 got through out of 72. Anyway, the remnants of the Battalion were strong enough to hold off yet another attack around dawn this morning. Brigade H.Q. is catching quite a lot of their big stuff which is sailing right over us, and I'm sorry to hear that Malcolm Dunbar has been wounded again. I should very much like to see a newspaper. No information at all as to the general state of affairs since this last lot started. I think that the fascists, by their usual concentration of artillery and avion (which works, for example, the way it worked here when the boys decided they could not stand any more of it, only usually the fascists are quicker to follow up) I think they have advanced for a depth of 4 or 5 kilometres on a Front probably 8 kilometres or so in length, left and right and through Corbera, which they now have again. I wonder why, when we take a village, we don't bring up a ton of dynamite and blow up the bloody church? Having retaken the town the fascists have put two machine-guns in the turret commanding a hell of a lot of territory. And, like most of these churches, it's strong enough to stand a lot of shelling.*

12th September. What the hell is this—we have moved out! The whole Brigade. Got the order to pack and were relieved somewhere around 2 A.M. Marched back and are now in the small hills, just off the road, half way between the Flix crossroads and Mora de Ebro. But, however good it is to have a break, I can't help feeling that we have not finished yet. For one thing, the Division is not out, only our 15th Brigade. Their bloody heavy artillery comes over too near, and their avion bombed the next valley this morning. There is an authentic sounding rumour that the first (and only) batch of chaps to go on Home Leave are still in Barcelona.

I'm sorry to say that Ben Glazer died in the ambulance. What grim ironic fate. It was arranged that he should stay back in what everybody thought was a safe spot, because of the state he was in and then—a shell which in theory just could not get there, did so. Poor old Ben; he won't play at Unity Theatre again.

By the way, they made up for a relatively quiet day just before we left by another fierce attack on the Lincolns. Like the rest, it was driven back, but it was hectic for an hour or so with some artillery landing down the valley also. The thought of yet another lot starting up made the troops move out pretty smartly when we did get the order to get going!

13th September. It seems the Captain was very pleased with us for going up with him that afternoon. He ought to be, too!

Later. What did I tell you? We have got a stand-by order already. A concentration of Italian troops has been spotted outside Corbera. We are just beginning to get some idea of what was happening when we all made that camion dash to the Front. Apparently things were pretty serious for awhile, but fortunately the speed with which the Brigade moved and got into position averted what might have been a critical situation. Then again, the next day (no, the one after) when we had our own private bit of excitement, Brigade H.Q. could not find out what was happening. Every telephone line was cut by the shelling, and runners sent up to the 24th and the Lincolns gave up trying to get through the barrage, gave a wild guess and went back reporting all sorts of things. What really took place was that some of the 24th who were then on that much-attacked hill on our left, and some of the Lincolns on our right, ran back. The Company, between the two, saw this and some of them followed suit in mild panic, leaving everything. So that it was a really good piece of work on the Captain's part to get them all back again before the fascists could follow up. With those hills in his possession, Franco could have forced a general withdrawal along a lengthy Front.

14th September. We have not moved yet. Maybe that Italian Division has melted away. Cold and wet today. We are sitting under a groundsheet which is lacking in the one essential of any groundsheet—waterproofing.

Later. The weather has cleared, and we once more have the hot sun. It has, so far, been quiet, not much avion coming around (they bombed us heavily yesterday) and with only a little shelling things are nice and peaceful. For how long, oh Lord, how long?

Later still. A very nasty finish. Late this evening they suddenly got bang on, with four shells, and one of the Company was wounded.

15th September. Here's hoping those damned Italians mutinied! Rumours are again rife. It seems pretty definite that the first batch of "leaves" were still in Barcelona two or three days ago, anyway. But now we hear that they have left and another batch will be following in a few days. I wonder. To-day we have had more spasmodic shelling; not more wounded from the Company but three men and five mules farther along the crest. What little tranquility there was around here has gone now, definitely.

16th September. Letters (and fags) coming through once more. Reasonably quiet to-day. Now it must be nearly supper time, i.e., more beans, for the sun has gone down behind our crest and the shadows are creeping up the hill of pines across the other side of this narrow valley. "And all the air a solemn stillness holds . . . ." I guess it will be beans. Hold everything, but to-day has been wonderfully quiet. Into the clearing in the valley comes the Propaganda Van which will, I presume, give us some music after supper. The last time they were up they invited anyone who wished to sing over the mike to step foward to do so: a Yank from the Lincolns came up and gave us—"I want to go Home."

17th September. A beautiful day, the kind of day one would like to have a holiday on, or even a Saturday afternoon would do. To amble gently on the bike, never exceeding 10 mph unless you were going down a steep hill, to stop as you wished at any pub you chose and lounge around outside with a pint of shandy and a cigarette. To go off down the lanes and pause a while watching the farm workers (for it is undoubtedly sweeter, on holiday, to see others working). Well, anyway, that is the kind of day it is—leaving out the millions of flies which are everywhere.

The Brigade got 250-300 recruits last night, all Spanish. They are said to be conscripts. The Lincolns got 50 of them. In the light of recent events, changes must be apparent in the general balance of things. Although the French border is officially closed there is reason to believe that some material is getting through to the Republic. Add to this, the unrest caused by Franco's rejection of the Withdrawal Plan, the Czech position, Chamberlain's compromising behaviour, and the chances of at least forcing the hand of the reactionaries increases daily. This morning's Spanish papers say that Chamberlain has flown to Germany "to confer with Hitler." Jesus Christ!

Later. There goes another one. Chris Smith, our Sergeant, is being sent as second-in-command of a new Anti-tank Battery (Spanish mostly, but with some Internationals, though not British). It seems this new Battery was not doing too well. During the last action—their first—they lost one gun. Now the Commander and the Political Commissar are being removed. Alan Gilchrist, the last Commissar our old Battery had, is to be the new Political Commissar; don't know who will be in Command. So now we are two, just Hughie Smith and me. Somehow it seems to make the atmosphere more oppressive.

Later still. We have just heard the second batch of Leaves are definitely going in a day or two, and that Chris Smith is one of them. I hope this Anti-tank job does not queer the pitch for him. To-day we have had a lot of avion, bloody close, and there is rather more artillery around the Front. These are the usual indications of another attempted push being in the offing. Who knows? Maybe those Italians were only tired and needed a rest first.

18th September. Chris has gone over to the Battery strongly hoping he will spend only one night there. I hope so, too, for the sooner this lot goes the sooner it will be our turn. Meanwhile there is too much activity for my liking. Their artillery continues, not very heavy but steady and consistent, very disturbing. Also we have already had a visit from their avion, mixing leaflets with bombs!

19th September. And then there was one— At least, there very soon will be, for the other Smith, Hughie, is going to the Commissariat to do the sketches for Our Fight. *So then I shall hold sway as the last of the Anti-tanks—in the machine-gunners! I am not overjoyed at the prospect, but after giving it some thought I have decided to stay where I am for the time being anyway. Or rather, I mean that I am not going to make any application for a change. I could transfer to the British Battalion but frankly I am wondering if that would not adversely affect my chance of Leave (assuming it ever* does *start again) for the Battalion has its own applicants. Chris says that the new Battery is full of Frenchmen and Italians who have been out here for a long time and who all want leave. So although I shall be the only International in this Company, with the exception of the two officers, I think I'll take a chance and stay where I am.*

This is a nuisance having to write in pencil again, but my pen is out of action once more. I shall try to hang on to the pen, though, for it came from Madrid.

Developments! Alan Gilchrist has just arrived and wants me to go to the new Anti-tank Battery as his Deputy Political Commissar! This alters things somewhat. He is going to see John Gates, Brigade Political Commissar, to arrange details. And at the moment our avion is about and we are having to keep our heads down because of the shrapnel from their *anti-aircraft guns. There's a pain in the neck from everything these days.*

Later. Bloody avion (90% theirs) has been the order of the day. Hughie Smith has gone now, so I'm the monarch of all I survey—for the moment. I do not expect to hear about my transfer until tomorrow. And even if I don't go, Levine, the Company Captain, says he will put me in his H.Q., which means I will at least have him to talk to.

20th September. Chris Smith called in for a chat. Afterwards I saw Alan Gilchrist who said it was all arranged for me to go to the new Battery, but I must wait for the formal transfer, probably tomorrow. This is rather a disappointment, I was hoping to get away to-night. This place is getting too darned hot for my liking.

The Battery, by the way, is definitely in the Line with their guns in position. It will be "before daylight, after-dark" feeding again of course, for they are well down the road to Corbera.

There has obviously been a battle to-day, and the British and Mac-Paps are already in action. So the battle is on again and we are again

part of it. What exactly has happened I do not know, but I do know for
sure that the 12th Brigade has lost two hills. The artillery and avion on
those two hills were very intense.

21st September. Midday. Settled my transfer, said goodbye to Levine
and my bloody rifle, bayonet, bullets, grenades and trench-mortar bombs
and, after an adventurous journey due to avion, located the Battery H.Q.

I do not recall any great elation at this belated promotion to Deputy
Political Commissar! My reaction was of a more practical kind. Finding
myself deprived of all the comrades with whom I had shared so much for
so long, my last day or two in the Machine-gun Company had not been
over happy ones. Now I was delighted and relieved—especially with the
increasing evidence of yet another spell of action being highly likely—to
be sharing whatever lay ahead with Chris and Alan once more. I had
always liked and respected both of them. On another, less worthy level, I
had joyfully shed the trappings of an infantryman for what I hoped would
be a less arduous role physically. Immodestly, I did not doubt that I would
acquit myself if not with honor, at least not dishonorably. The next few
days were to present a test greater than any we International Brigaders had
known so far.

In London, Paris, Prague, Berlin and Rome decisions were being
reached, agreements made—integrity and human dignity forgotten—
which would mock the bravery, the sacrifices, and the suffering of the
Spanish and Czech peoples. Affected as we were by immediate events,
hopes still riding high on the initial success of this offensive, we had no
real inkling of the approaching climax of the drama of Spain. We were
well aware of the ferocity of the fascist counter attacks, the ground they
had regained, the frightful casualties we had suffered. But we were still
across the Ebro, still capable of fighting valiantly and to good purpose.
More troops and guns had come up, our avion was around. France had
reopened its border, or was daily expected to do so. The list of hopeful
signs was long, if you wanted to find them. We saw no end to this battle
except in victory; the end by then determined in other capitals of the
world presaged the death of the Spanish Republic.

21st September (contd). There is an intense battle going on at present in our sector. Our anti-tank guns are farther up the crest, and covering the Corbera road. Their planes have been over three times and their artillery is bashing away.

Have met the Captain (Battery Commander, a Frenchman); seems a decent guy. So now I'm officially installed. There has been a heavy fascist attack aided by their usual concentration of heavy artillery, much of which hit around here, making us very thankful for our dug-outs. But the latest news from Brigade is that the fascists have made no advance. They say we attacked last night and took back one of the two hills captured yesterday from the 12th Brigade. But they are evidently making another big push on us here. Poor old 15th Brigade catches it again.

22nd September. 9 A.M. A lousy night. This bloody dug-out is alive with fleas! The Brigade Commander, Major Valledor, was here a few minutes ago. No more developments yet. Seems funny (!) how the Brigade sort of slipped into action this time—but it eased the blow. Anyway, as I might have said before, once in the Line you can cease all speculation about leave etc., and feel quite a bit more at ease. (Don't misunderstand that bit; it's not a plea for more Front Line action!)

About 3 P.M. Had a very terrific bombing, and this was the signal for the battle to begin again. I bet their artillery is as much as in the Great War. It really is frightening and thoroughly lousy. No. 3 gun phoned to report troops had been seen retreating from a hill to the right which was under heavy shell fire. Chris and I made it up to them pronto, but it seemed to be just a few individuals. We could do nothing other than pass on the information to Brigade. More avion.

23rd September. More excitement. And, I regret, another advance of the fascists who took another hill after altering its shape and reducing its height by shells and bombs. The Brigade, except us, has moved. The Battalions have taken up positions of the 13th Brigade, which we were in last with the Machine-gun Company. We stay where we are since our guns are in excellent situation for any tank attack. Alan has now named me as his official replacement as Commissar should he get knocked out. The sinister part of this is that we were in precisely the same position, he and I, at Teruel, with the old Battery; only it was I who got knocked out!

Funny incident. Levine has told Alan Gilchrist that if asked for com-
mendations he would name Chris and me, for going up with him that
afternoon . . . .

Later. Whilst nothing exactly critical has occurred to-day, yet I think
the situation is quite serious. The day began with the usual accompani-
ment of avion and heavy shelling. When the latter was at its worst in the
sector immediately ahead, our No. 1 gun told us that troops were leaving
the hill in front, then that the Lincolns too were retreating. At the same
time the telephone lines to the Brigade and the Lincolns went dead. We
could not find out from any reliable authority what was happening, but
we could see for ourselves that our troops, believed to be the Lincolns,
were retreating towards our No. 1 gun. We had no alternative but to pull
the gun out to the hill behind. Meanwhile our heavy artillery was work-
ing overtime and I think saved the situation. Anyway, the fascists were
stopped from making any further advance. For a while, comparative
quiet, while we heard various accounts of what had happened. It seems
that, after their usual heavy bombardment, they were able to infiltrate
between hills and half surround some of the Lincolns and the Machine-
gun Company (What a lucky escape for me!) which was with them. The
whole Lincoln Battalion was forced to withdraw with, we hear, some 40-
50 losses, mostly from the Machine-gun Company, but whether killed,
captured, or merely strayed, they are not sure.

One delicious rumour, and one piece of news. Rumour: no Spanish
papers allowed over the River Ebro yesterday (we got none) because
Premier Negrin has announced in Geneva the immediate withdrawal of
all Internationals!!! News (heard by listening in to a phone conversation
of the Divisional Commander): there are revolts against Franco in
Morocco and Burgos. Can it be true?

It was understandable that the Army High Command should want to
suppress Negrin's announcement at least until intention could be trans-
lated into fact. But the way in which we were able to listen in to the
Divisional Commander and promptly spread that particular piece of nonsense (as of course it proved to be) illustrated the impossibility of with-
holding such a traumatic development as the imminent war's end for
every International.

Our impending withdrawal was soon known to all. Yet such was the
critical position at the Front that for that day and part of the night the

British Battalion, and indeed the whole 15th Brigade, were called upon to endure some of the hardest fighting of the offensive.

24th September.

25th September. I could not have written a word yesterday to save my life, for quite seriously for some while life had very little in it to interest me.

Imagine, if you can, our feelings on the night of the 23rd when, not merely the 15th Brigade but the whole 35th International Division was relieved, not just to go into reserve but straight back across the River and we, just the bloody Anti-tank Battery, were left here in the Line, attached to the relieving troops, the Campesinos.

I tell you, I was simply broken up, and Chris was too. This was proof positive that the rumour of Negrin's speech at Geneva announcing the immediate withdrawal of all Internationals was not a rumour, but is perfectly true.

The night waned, and day began again, another of those inter-minable, ghastly days. The last of the departing troops marched back down the road before dawn and we were left. The Brigade Commander had not yet gone and Alan Gilchrist and the Battery Captain rushed off to see him. But all he said was that he would see the Division Commander. Then they went to see the Brigade Commander of the Campesinos—he would speak to his own Division. Smith (another of them, a Lieutenant with the H.Q. of our own Division now, but an old pal of ours) as Liaison Officer had been delayed in leaving, and he came to see us and said he would be certain to see our own Divisional Commander when he got back to Marsa. (Just think, that's where the 15th Brigade is now) and I'm sure he will. This cheered us up a little, but we needed all our fortitude when the bombers came over later and the battle went on again. Somehow the day ended. Maybe, sometime when circumstances are more propitious, I'll write the Edgar Allan Poe story of the real agony of it, but now I can't because it hasn't ended yet. About mid-morning we phoned the Campesinos, no news. So that was that. Obviously we are here for another day. The Captain and Alan went off in our kitchen truck to Marsa, to see our own Brigade, but our lack of faith was justified by the fact that we are still here and, quite obviously, staying the day. True, they saw John Gates, 15th Brigade Political Commissar, who said this would probably be our last day here, but so many shocks have we had we feel the chances of this being true would be greater if the whole Brigade was still here, not just we few. Gates has had enough too. Still, there's always old Tom Paine: "These are the times to try men's souls. The Summer Patriot and the Sunshine Soldier will fail, but the men who, in this hour of crisis stand by their Country, deserve the love and thanks of all men and women." Take it out of that if you can!

By the way, the story of the 23rd, last day in action of the 15th Brigade, was, I'm afraid, a somewhat inglorious one. This is not to be wondered at, for the Brigade was tired out and more or less finished by seven weeks of terrible fighting even before it went in again for the last time. But they did go in again and it was only by sheer luck that no large-scale rout took place, so we were told by Lieutenant Smith. In the morning the Lincolns were subjected to an intense bombardment and were forced to retire. They were, however, kept together and took up positions on the hill behind. Later, during the afternoon, the British and the Mac-Paps, on the left of the road, got the same shelling and bombing whilst in completely inadequate trenches, and simply left in disorder. This was where the luck came in, for the fascists, for some reason, did not follow up, merely moving on to the hills that had been vacated. This gave time to bring up reinforcements, so that their gains were not too great. But what might have happened is pretty bad to think about; or, for that matter, what almost certainly would have happened had the Division not been relieved during that night, for the 11th and 13th Brigades are more or less in the same state as the 15th.

There was one good point about last night. Chris Smith and I have had virtually no sleep for three nights what with general excitements—and fleas. Last night, whether we moved or not, something had to be done, for snatches of sleep during the daytime are even more impossible than at night, and we were exhausted. So we got the seats out of a car which had been blown up in the bombing, placed them outside our dug-out, shook the fleas out of our blankets, or most of them, and had a damned good sleep for all of three hours, in spite of the fact that it rained steadily. Of course, in our exalted positions Chris and I don't do guard duty, though we go our rounds of the guns regularly. This morning it is dull and raining off and on, the clouds are low, so perhaps their troops will be discouraged from attacking and their bombers unable to fly! In this way, we might perhaps be allowed to pass an uneventful day until dark—then perhaps we shall be relieved. But I doubt it.

Later. Sure enough, we have had a quiet day. It rained steadily for most of it and not a plane came over, and only a few shells. Went round the guns with Chris. So, somehow, the day ended, but don't ask me how.

26th September. Of course we are still here, and with yet another bloody day in front of us. Just as Chris and I expected, no relief showed up during the night so back again to Marsa went the Captain and Alan. They returned with the most incredible piece of news. It seems that according to Division the Battery has definitely to remain in position and so our Brigade Commander is arranging for the Captain, Gilchrist and me to be withdrawn, and the rest—when it can be arranged! We (Chris and myself, anyway) are beyond refusing to take advantage of this, but the injustice must be obvious, particularly since the majority of the Battery are Internationals, mostly French. So now, about 10 A.M., Alan and the Captain have gone back yet again to fix details and we are waiting, waiting, waiting through another endless morning. They should be back about 12 or 1 P.M., and then maybe we can really and truly go. Can it be true?

I have just been the rounds of the guns and from No. 3 gun taken what I sincerely hope will be my last ever look at Corbera, half veiled in the mist which this morning envelopes everything, though still with that cursed church tower standing out clear and distinct, symbol, it seems to me, of all the vileness of this whole offensive. Corbera Church; why write it again? As though I could ever forget it.

Later. About 7 P.M. Now the Captain has returned, alone. He has some results. The latest now is that all *Internationals from our Battery are being relieved tonight (about 18 in all), the Brigade is sending up 15 replacements, Spaniards, new recruits, I believe. That is something—even though he did say, as an afterthought, "To-night or tomorrow." Of course it will be tomorrow*

27th September. Still here. Alan Gilchrist did not return yesterday, so I suppose I am Political Commissar right now! I guess we have another day of this, and I bet it's a hectic one out of sheer cussedness.

Later. About 5 P.M. The High Command is a wonderful thing. Not only did they not choose to send the relief during the night or very early morning, nor were they content to send it up merely in daylight—they had to send it right in the middle of a battle. Chris and I were having a nasty time, for the Captain went off early some place and did not return.

Soon, their artillery opened up, the bombers came over, and the battle was on once more. Our last day! Then the inevitable happened: "Troops retreating on the right!" Chris, however, never lacking courage despite his desire, equal to mine, to get the hell out of this, sorted things out and restrained our gunners from retreating. So it went on.

And I, incidentally, perforce saw Corbera yet again. Then suddenly about 4 P.M., a truck and a gang of chaps appeared—relief for the Anti-tanks! But why, just to look a gift-horse in the mouth for a moment, did it have to come in the middle of the battle and when the Captain was not there? Obviously we couldn't simply re-arrange the gun crews etc., collect up the Internationals, and scram without waiting for the Captain Where the hell was he, anyway? The truck driver wanted to get back at once, but we would not let him go. Then we decided it was far too risky keeping truck and men hanging around in here, what with frequent bombing raids and plenty of shelling. So finally, with half a dozen or so Internationals from the guns, I went back with it and them, making the driver wait at our Battery kitchen.

I am sitting outside the kitchen now, regretting a little (hypocrite!) that I left Chris, though he expected to follow me pretty soon. To think that in a few hours the War will be over for us.

Battery kitchen is on the Mora de Ebro road, about 3 kilometres short of Mora. A very old Spanish woman has just come out of a nearby half-ruined house. Together we watch and listen to the shells falling along a wide range of the hills I have just left. "Not near?" she asked, wanting reassurance. "Not near," I told her, and wondered silently how long it would be before they were much closer. It is about 6.30 pm, and Chris is due any minute, I'm glad to say.

I'm even more glad to say, now, that Chris arrived safely with the remaining Internationals, Frenchmen and a few Italians, those who had not come back with me. Our reunion was a happy one, though we had been apart for no more than a few hours. Somberly, sadness and joyous relief making a hash of our emotions, we hitched a lift and re-crossed the River Ebro. If either of us wondered what had been achieved since we went over on that pontoon bridge on the 26th of July, the thought remained unspoken.

28th September. Gourmets, a village near Marsa. And now at last it has all ended, including the worst four days of my life.

We were now, all Internationals, back again this side of the River
Ebro. The psychological effect of having re-crossed the river was tremen-
dous—as great in the relief it brought as the elation it had given us all
when we had gone over in July. "That" side was the War. Now,
inevitably, we began to think of safety and home. There was noticeably
less bravura among us; those few who wanted to talk of their own self-
less deeds found only rare listeners. The horrors of the seven-week long
Battle of the Ebro had left us all drained of emotion. Our bitter disap-
pointment at not being able to achieve a decisive victory was com-
pounded by a common gut feeling that the battle was already lost when
we left it, that once again a great Republican offensive promising so
much at its beginning had been held and turned. Yet I am confident I do
no man an injustice in my conviction that this escape—unsought by
us—from death and the ever-present fear of death was dominant in our
minds as we left the War.

The sun was shining, the day already warm, as our party of old men and
women left the small coastal town of San Carlos for this bittersweet return
to the Ebro battlefields. But as we neared the River, dark clouds covered
the sky, a chilly wind blew up. It seemed to us fitting that though most of
those horrific seven weeks had been unrelieved scorching sun, we should
see the hills and crags once so ominous under this somber sky, for it had
been a hard and dark time.

From the coach windows, I saw a sign: "To Corbera." Soon we were
driving through the village, looking left and right in a futile effort to recognize this larger and largely rebuilt church and its tower. Then Corbera was
behind us and as we ascended the surrounding rugged, tortuous hills, I
almost came to doubt what I knew for a fact, that I had once climbed,
dragged a gun and fought over a fair number of them.

Then the coach could go no farther. A rough, rock-strewn track lay
ahead. But age and our many disabilities prevented us, now making our
slow and painful way on foot, from reaching the highest slopes and, in particular, Hill 481. We were compelled to stop still some distance from the
top.

Part of the Sierra de Pandols, Hill 481 had proved the barrier to further advance by the Republican troops. What anguish and how many
lives those repeated attacks cost! And even now we were unable, this

time prevented by years and many infirmities, to reach the positions and gun emplacements we had once clung to near, so very near, the crest.

In the familiar arid terraces of olive groves and orderly rows of grape bushes, we gathered around Bill Alexander. There was a sad task to perform. Bill spoke first, while the television crews quietly recorded the scene. Chris Smith, my anti-tank comrade with whom, on these same hills, I had spent many harrowing days and nights, took from him a small casket wrapped in a red scarf borrowed from my wife, Sadie, and, on the lower slopes of 481 we scattered the ashes of Alan Gilchrist, who had played a valiant part in this and other battles. Sadly, Alan was cheated by death two weeks before this long-awaited return. Like the rest, standing silent and bareheaded, I had my memories of considerate, cheerful Alan. Foolishly I reproached myself for having once snapped at him. One early morning somewhere around Teruel in mid-January, I was in a trench, filthy, tired, cold and hungry. The day before had been a bad one and there was little reason to suppose this one would be much better. Alan, whose never failing good humor was a source of great comfort to all of us, came along on his rounds. He was then, I think, Political Commissar to us Anti-tanks. With what was, perhaps, just a touch too frivolous in the circumstances, he chuckled "My God, Fred, you *do* look a mess." I could only glower at him and snarl "What the hell do you think you look like?" I can see his face now, a mixture of genuine regret that he should be, though inadvertently, unkind to a comrade, and his own hurt that I could imagine he had spoken with intent. But soon we were both laughing. I remember him with affection.

My wife was in tears. Somewhere on these hills her twenty-one year old brother, Max Nash, had died in one of the many futile and costly attacks. The whereabouts of his grave, if grave he was allowed by the final victors, was unknown. Red carnations were placed at the foot of an olive tree, a bold splash of color against the brown earth. Then we forty-odd British sang the "International," and remembered our dead comrades.

One lone, elderly farm worker watched these strange proceedings. He too stood bareheaded, holding his beret in his hands until the end. Then he moved away, climbing with little apparent effort high above us to continue the daunting task of wresting yet another narrow terrace from the steep hillside. In his, or perhaps his son's good time, one more row of olive trees would yield fruit.

There was less chattering than usual as we returned in the coach. Now, as then, Hill 481 had left its mark.

VII

October-December, 1938
Repatriation

From the day Prime Minister Negrin announced the withdrawal of all International Brigade volunteers, our continued presence in Spain became another burden on the desperately struggling Republic. There were several thousand of us: we had to be fed, precious fuel and transport used to serve our needs. But in the more than two frustrating months before we British finally went home we were treated individually and collectively as, in Pasionaria's words, "Honored guests."

A few days after coming out of the Line, the 15th International Brigade became an all-Spanish Brigade and at once left to return to the Ebro and the battle. Barnardo, Montesinos, and Eduardo bade Chris and me affectionate farewells and went with the rest. We had gone through much together; as we embraced, we knew we would probably never meet again. In 1984 an advertisement in the Spanish press for any news of our three comrades brought one reply only. Barnardo's brother wrote to tell me that Barnardo was killed four days after re-joining the battle. Of Montesinos and Eduardo I have heard nothing, nor, indeed, of any other of our Spanish comrades.

In those months of waiting most of us experienced the extremes of emotion, of great hope and dark depression. A series of farewell parades began almost at once and, while these seemed inescapably to involve us in considerable physical inconvenience, we were deeply affected by the obviously sincere friendship shown us by the Spanish people.

From the BBC we learnt that Hitler had given Czechoslovakia two days to agree to his territorial demands. I doubt if many of us appreciated the true significance of what, later, became the Munich crisis. Czechoslovakia, betrayed and helpless, gave in. We found no comfort for the Spanish people in Chamberlain's actions.

We were also painfully aware of the daily lack of encouraging news from our own war. At Marsa the guns on the Ebro Front sounded just a bit nearer each day; then, clearly audible, the chatter of machine-guns. Communiques in the Spanish press spoke of heroic resistance—day after day resistance was the key word. We thought of our Spanish comrades still there, and feared for them.

As if to underline the fact that repatriation was still a long way off, short leaves to Barcelona were arranged. On 12th October it was my turn. I found the City hungrier, more serious, more concerned than it had seemed a few months before, though the Ramblas was still full of evening promenaders and pretty girls.

I gave one day to revisiting Mataró Hospital and there I met Renee and Isobel again. Both were looking forward to returning soon to their native New Zealand. But, surprise surprise—Renee has married Willy, the German lad, also a long-standing patient at Huete. Surely they will have problems? Will he be allowed into her country? I'm damned sure he won't want to go back to Germany! Isobel is very critical and disapproving of her friend, but privately. I felt that her concern was mostly due to the fact (so she says) that Renee is thirty eight years old and Willy only twenty four! Anyway, it was good to see them again and talk over old times. I wished them good luck and, to Renee, what encouragement I could, and then had to leave.

16th October. Getting back to Marsa was quite an experience! The train was so overcrowded that with many more I had to ride on the roof, an extremely unpleasant, uncomfortable and filthy way of travelling, and it lasted several hours. Three times actual or rumoured air attacks kept the train in tunnels for lengthy periods, steam and smoke leaving us soaked and choking. I finally made Marsa at 3 A.M. and went straight to sleep, dirt and all.

Our fears for the outcome of the Ebro battle were somewhat allayed on reading that "Our troops have taken two hills in the Sierra de Pandols, advanced slightly on the right, and are now in a position for cutting off the Fascist salient." Meanwhile we still heard the guns just as clearly and as loud.

According to the BBC, Mussolini is willing to withdraw 10,000 "volunteers" from Spain. That would be just about the number he has here in sick and wounded, anyway.

As in all of Republican Spain, hunger was a major weapon on Franco's side. In Marsa swarms of children and even some adults, mostly women, waited patiently outside the church where we were fed hoping for scraps from our meal. One day the BBC announced that fascist planes had bombed Barcelona with loaves of bread, together with leaflets exhorting the population to come over to their side for "Peace, Bread and Work." If true, the bread would be acceptable!

With no further reference in the press to our forces' threat to the fascist salient, the theme of "fierce resistance" was resumed.

We finally left Marsa for good on 24th October, in the dark figuratively as well as literally, and in the middle of a torrential rainstorm. Two days later we arrived at Ripoll, in northern Spain. Much of the intervening time our bedraggled and miserable crowd sat shivering in saturated clothes in slow-moving or stationary trains. The remaining time was spent in yet another Grand Parade, this one honored by the whole Army Council. Making a gallant effort to rise to the occasion we cheered our heads off, much to the gratification of the many press photographers present from many countries. But it was too wet for the planned March Past, and we British eventually went to sit once more in the waiting train. It was still raining.

27th October. Ripoll, about 35 kilometres from the French border and 107 north of Barcelona. This is where we are to spend our last days/weeks in Spain. They marched us to the church, a large one of course, and gave us bread, a very peculiar and previously unknown kind of sausage and—cocoa! Unsweetened.

Later we British paraded in a field where Malcolm Dunbar stressed that military discipline would continue to be enforced etc., etc. Johnny Gates, an American and Brigade Political Commissar, added more to the same effect. He then added that we would be returning to Barcelona tomorrow for the biggest and last Farewell Parade, from the people of Spain to all Internationals. A few of the habitual moaners were true to form and grumbled about the long hours spent on such occasions waiting about in trains for hours at a time getting nowhere, but the great majority welcomed the news. There's something very satisfying to the ego about these Parades!

Friday 28th October. This Parade had better be good! Up at 3am, then to the church for "coffee" and bread. On the train at 6.30 and departed at twenty minutes to nine. We reached Barcelona at 1 oclock and were brought here to the Lenin Barracks by trucks. at 2 oclock we have had some food and are now awaiting developments.

Saturday 29th October. Yesterday was a day I will never forget. The Parade was, I am sure, an emotional feast for us all. It was no simple march through the streets, but a glorious demonstration of the enthusiasm and affection of the people of Catalonia for the Internationals.

Trucks took us through crowded streets, with flags and bunting everywhere, the people cheering and throwing flowers, crowding every window and balcony. We dismounted finally at the Sarria Road, starting point of the procession.

There the Brigades of many different nationalities were drawn up nine abreast. Spanish troops lined the route as, led by military bands, we set off. Everywhere thousands packed the broad streets, time after time men and women broke through the cordon to hug and kiss us, holding up small children and babies to be kissed in return, smothering us with affection as they cheered and cheered.

For an hour and a half we made our slow way through some of the principle streets in one long glut of emotional excess. I was not the only Brigader sometimes reduced to tears: we, who were leaving the fight, were yet receiving the heartfelt homage of the Spanish people.

In the Street of the 14th of April the March ended, and then came the speeches. From a platform full of important people from many countries as well as of the Republic, Dr. Negrin, Prime Minister, addressed us and the vast crowds. Then came President Azaña followed by the Chief of the Army of the Ebro. Finally we recognised the spare figure of the indomitable "La Pasionaria" who quickly had the crowd roaring their approval of her every word. But we British were not near enough to hear much, so I have had to wait until to-day to read her stirring speech: one sentence stands out—"Come back, as honoured Sons of Spain."

Then it was over. As dusk was falling the Parade dispersed. Trucks were parked in nearby streets and we were taken back to the Lenin Barracks to eat.

The train ride back to Ripoll saw us all come down to earth. We boarded about 7 P.M., left Barcelona two hours later, and reached Ripoll, about sixty-five miles, at 8 o'clock next morning. By that time we were all very, very cold, tired and hungry. But at Ripoll there was no food since we had been expected at 2 A.M. So, instead, we slept.

There were no more Parades, no more Grand Fiestas, only occasional rather half-hearted efforts to organise our own concerts. Life became a little tougher each day, with further deterioration in rations and increasing cold—the Pyrenees were not so very far away now and many were forced to go about wrapped in their sleeping blanket for some protection against the biting winds. It was still dark when we marched to the church for breakfast, and dark again by mid-afternoon, though some days saw bright, warm sunshine for a few hours.

As the emotional stress of battle and our sudden release therefrom receded, and with no tangible evidence of impending repatriation, we were in danger of some despondency. The signs of chronic food shortages were everywhere. Virtually nothing could be bought in the shops or cafes other than the customary ersatz black coffee, over which we sat for hours in the long evenings. Almost daily we read that, Heavy fighting was continuing on the Ebro Front and were left to make what we would of that bald statement.

It would be hypocrisy to pretend that we British regretted our involuntary withdrawal from the fighting. When, suddenly and unexpected, the Government ordered us out of the battle and the war, we excused our immense relief by the bland assertion that the Republican Army was now judged strong enough to stand on its own, no longer in need of the International Brigades' aid to achieve final victory. This was, of course, another illusion to add to the many we had nurtured throughout the war, based on hope and dedication to our cause rather than on fact or even probability. The true reason for the Government's decision, in no way dishonorable, was political It was Negrin's last throw in his constant endeavors to win support from other countries in this war against fascism. Like all previous attempts it failed because the purblind democracies preferred Hitler and Mussolini. It was as simple as that. But our explanation helped assuage the unease our new role as bystanders caused us. Yet one part of each man wanted still to help in Spain's fight for survival. But as the weeks dragged by we wanted, one and all, to go home. We waited, becoming less soldier-like each day. Then came a glimmer of hope.

Wednesday, 2nd November. It's here! The League of Nations Commission is really here. Their job is to supervise the withdrawal of all Volunteers. We British paraded this morning and behold, there they all were in all their glory. There was a red-braided British General, he's the big chief, a colonel from Denmark, another from Sweden, a British Captain and a Mr. Field, an American.

The General addressed us and managed to leave a nasty taste in our mouths right away by what sounded like an invitation to tell them any dirt we could, nature not specified, and in confidence, of course. There was a comic side too, though, for they were all gloriously attired in their respective immaculate uniforms—except Mr. Field was in civvies—and the British pair with appropriate accents. Their thoughts when confronted with the many 'gorblimey' members of our rag-tag and bobtail army must have been very upsetting. By then many no longer bothered even to try to shave, and about the only uniformity of our dress was a general concern for warmth.

Anyway they all sat at their tables, we all filed past giving a few basic details of name, our home town, then they gave each a cigarette and that was that.

The immediate result of this activity was to kid most of us simple souls into thinking that we were as good as on our way home. Two days later the Commission packed it bags and left, and we sank back into reality.

Later that week the Spanish press reported more withdrawals on the Ebro Front. But then to offset this we read of "a splendid Govt victory just north of Lerida in which the River Segre has been crossed and two towns captured." Once again we hoped: could this be the diversion that would force Franco into relieving the pressure on the Ebro? No more was heard of it. As before, bulletins reverted to the all-too familiar terse and comfortless, "Intense fighting continues on the whole length of the Front."

At Ripoll I had met up with an old Labour Party friend, Frank Farr. Neither had known the other was in Spain. Frank had received a rare parcel including some even rarer bars of soap! Weather permitting, Frank and I got out into the countryside. Driven by necessity (not shared by all) on some brighter days we took an all-over wash in the river, afterwards belting up and down like mad to restore some circulation to our frozen bodies.

No word came of our departure. We did hear, however, that the British Consul was supposed to be visiting us, but no one seemed to know for what purpose. Telegrams were sent off to a number of sympathetic M.P.'s back home demanding action. Even the most committed among us were becoming frustrated and angry.

Then on a day whose cold and wet beginning was emphasised by the absence of any food at all at breakfast time, came a far greater gloom.

17th November. Spanish papers to-day confirm—or rather, admit that our troops have had to retire to this side of the River Ebro. In other words to the positions we held on the 24th of July. The retirement, they say, was an orderly withdrawal with no losses of men or material. I'm afraid that last bit sounds hard to believe.

It was a dreadful blow. The realization that after all the bloody fighting, every inch of ground won since the crossing of the Ebro on 25th July had been lost, brought sadness and, irrationally, a feeling of guilt.

Through pep talks and our own heartfelt endeavors we did our best to stand reality on its head. To us of the International Brigade, the Battle of the Ebro was a victory. How else to remember the many comrades killed, the torture of the long, frightful weeks? Despite what was perhaps, in hindsight, a losing battle from its beginning in July 1936, we saw this war as a triumphant vindication of all we believed about the inevitability of victory for the people's forces over the class enemies. We, the reality behind the dream of "Workers of the World Unite," had come to Spain to play our part in that victory and help to destroy fascism. But as cold as the icy waters of the river was the dread thought that we were leaving Spain and the Spanish people to carry on that fight alone. For each of us, as we longed for home, it was a nagging reproach.

Thursday, 17th November. Chamberlain and Daladier are to meet on the 23rd of this month to discuss "a solution of the Spanish question." No doubt Chamberlain, after already selling out Czechoslovakia, will use "General Franco's decisive victory" as a weapon to bully Daladier (if he needs it) to sell out the Spanish Republic. But they still won't find it easy. Though here it is reported that largo Caballero is again making trouble, attempting splitting tactics.

Thursday, 24th November. The Commission is back again! Rumours rife once more.

The British Government's lack of anxiety for our speedy return to Britain's shores made us all very angry. The days passed slowly amid increasing unease for both ourselves and events in Spain. Chamberlain, it was obvious, was little concerned about us or the Spanish Republic.

The customary report of Political Commissars at Front Line level "The morale of the troops remains high," was invariably the cause of much derision among those same troops. If Bob Cooney, the much-liked Political Commissar of the British Battalion, dared to use it publicly during our last two weeks or so, there might well have been a minor riot. The simple truth was we were all thoroughly sick of this seemingly endless and increasingly unpleasant day-to-day existence. More cables were sent to Britain, and on 29th November we heard that the *News Chronicle* was demanding we be brought home; also questions were to be asked in the House of Commons. Frank Farr and I went for another long walk.

Thursday, 1st December. News! "In reply to questions, the Under-Secretary for Foreign Affairs announced that the British volunteers in Spain would be returning to Britain within eight to ten days." So said the BBC broadcast last night.

This was confirmed by telegrams from Wilfred Roberts, M.P., and the British Consul in Barcelona stated we are to leave next Monday or Tuesday!!!

Sunday, 4th December. Everybody pretty excited. We leave on Tuesday. It has its comic side: the British Government has graciously agreed to grant us DBS—Distressed British Subject—status. Yesterday we all had to sign that we would repay the cost of the journey home! Some hopes. Getting a bath and some civvy clothes tomorrow. I have bought a shirt, socks and some underwear, all cheap and not good quality but all that was for sale in the few poor shops, and anyway it took nearly all my pesetas. Rumoured we might also be given overcoats, which will be more than welcome if it is half as cold in England as it is here now. I shant have many pesetas to change, but with luck if we go through France without stops I might manage ten shillings English money. Rather worried about getting these diaries through the censor—

we were told yesterday not to try to take out anything of the kind!
Local "Left Republicans" planning to give us a rousing send-off. We go
by train from Ripoll to the French border. All walking around in a
dream, now that it is actually happening.

We did get a bath—or, rather, a hot shower, of which we were all in
need, some more than others. Those cold baths Frank and I had taken
were not just exercises in Spartan endurance. Oddments of civilian jack-
ets, trousers and shoes were handed out, largely on a hit-or-miss method,
but no overcoats. Had I been another Jason Gurney that was my moment
to demand to know what they had done with my natty plus-four suit in
which I'd arrived twenty months before.[49] . . . I need not have worried
about spending my last few pesetas on high living in France. French police
sealed the train at the border and sped us on our way, though we were fed
very well indeed on the journey. My diaries were passed easily enough by
virtue of my having been appointed as Censor!

No one could have hoped for a more appreciative, more generous
farewell than we. Most of the populace turned out with flags and banners,
showing their feelings openly with tears as well as cheers. As our train
pulled out of the station, we saw as a last reminder of Spanish friendship,
elderly José of our favorite café waving his Left Republican flag and calling
out "Long live our British comrades. Long live the International Brigades!"
With almost unbelievable generosity we were each issued with a tin or
bully for the short journey to France; gladly I recall that nearly all was
handed back at the border.

So this small gesture of support was our last in Spain. In two and a half
years of bitter and bloody fighting we British volunteers left some hundreds of our comrades on the battlefields, their graves desecrated and
unmarked by the fascist victors. History will tell we lost many battles. We
know that the cause for which we fought and so many died, lived on. Less
than one year later the battle was at last joined between much of the free
world and the evil of Hitler fascism. Too late for a whole generation of
Spaniards, just in time for so many others.

On December 7th, 1938, the British Volunteers came home. At
Victoria Station, in darkness, thousands packed the surrounding streets to
greet us, and to recognize relative or friend among the dishevelled and
unshaven men, markedly unburdened with luggage after our long
absence. In unusual and soon-to-be disowned unity, Communist Party
chiefs Harry Pollitt and Willie Gallagher stood side by side with Sir

Stafford Cripps and Clem Attlee. Some speeches, some cheering, and we dispersed. I was lucky; friends claimed me and gave me needed hospitality. I wonder what I spent those ten shillings on! [50]

There were no medals to be won in Spain. But I believe that no man, not even that Band of Brothers who fought upon St. Crispins Day, nor that later Few of 1940, justly honored though they be, was ever prouder of his part than are we who were of the International Brigade.

Notes

The Fifteenth International Brigade

Throughout his tour of duty in Spain, Fred Thomas served with the XVth International Brigade, one of five such formations organized to support the beleagured Republic of Spain. The designation "International" signified that the rank and file and their officers were, indeed, not Spaniards but volunteers from abroad. The first of these brigades, the XIth, called the Thaelmann and the XIIth, the Garibaldi, appeared in the Battle of Madrid in October and November, 1936. By the end of that year, the XIIIth, Dombrowski and the XIVth, La Marseillaise, had come into the line. Each brigade comprised three to five or six infantry battalions which were themselves recruited along ethnic/national compositions. Of this quartet, the Thaelmann carried the reputation of the most aggressive with its high percentage of German anti-Naziis.

On or about 1 February 1937,the XVth International Brigade entered the war. The senior component was the British Battalion, mustered on 26 December 1936, its No.I company quickly taken from training and sent into action by the New Year. Subsequently, the American force called the Abraham Lincoln Battalion joinedthe brigade as did its brother,the George Washington Battalion, which took such casualties in its first campaign, the Battle of Brunete, that its survivors transferred into the Lincolns.

Another early recruit was the Sixth of February Battalion, a truly hybrid collection of Algerians, Greeks, Morrocans, Americans, Syrians, Hungarians and Israelis. Still another was the 24th (Spanish) Battalion composed of Latin-American,Cuban and Mexican volunteers. There was the Dimitrov Battalion, whose members came from the Balkans, Czechoslavakia, Poland, Austria and Italy. And there was the Mackenzie-Papineau Battalion, inspired by the presence of hundreds of Canadians. All of these battalions comprised the XVth International Brigade.

The British Anti-tank Battery which Thomas joined was a Brigade force, subject to orders given by Brigade headquarters.

Notes

1. Oswald Mosley, once a promising member of traditional British politics, organized the British Union of Fascists in the early 1930s and quickly established himself as an anti-semite, anti-communist, pro-Nazi demagogue.
2. Labour declined to argue against non-intervention and so aroused considerable wrath among supporters of the Spanish Republic.
3. The lines are the first stanza of John Galsworthy's "Errantry" published in his 1934 *Collected Poems*.
4. The "farce of nonintervention" is a reference to the Non Intervention Agreement orchestrated by Great Britain and France and involving two dozen other European nations. In an effort to prevent the civil war from spreading, these powers effectively ruined the cause of the Republic.
5. There were three Welsh sea-captains, all named Jones: "Potato,""Corn Cob," and "Ham and Eggs," whose ships were ordered by Whitehall to wait in St. Jean de Luz for orders regarding further passage to blockaded Bilbao. "Potato" Jones spoke saltily with the press about a proposed breakthrough but, after all, took his cargo to Valencia. *The Seven Seas Spray* under a Captain Roberts did make a successful voyage to Bilbao.
6. For the details concerning Spanish refugees in Great Britain, see Jim Fyrth's *The Signal Was Spain* (New York: St. Martins Press, 1986).
7. Coordinator of the recruitment of British volunteers was R. W. Robson, formerly National Organiser for the Party. His office was 1 Litchfield St, also the address of the I. B. Dependents' Aid Fund.
8. The British Foreign Enlistment Act of 1870 was invoked in January, 1937, as the government sought to intimidate prospective volunteers. In its original form, the act forbade enlistment by British nationals in the armed forces of a foreign state at war with a friendly (i.e. to Great Britain) foreign state. Penalties included imprisonment and and a fine.
9. Charlotte Haldane's account of her service in Paris is in her memoir, *Truth Will Out* (New York: The Vanguard Press, 1950).
10. Most volunteers were sent to Perpignan and from there were led by Spanish and French smugglers up and down devious paths over the Pyrenees Mountains and finally into Spain. On 29 May 1937, the *Ciudad de Barcelona* carrying several dozen Internationals, was torpedoed by an Italian submarine and sunk within sight of landfall. A number of volunteers died in the incident.

11. The "Anarchist trouble in Barcelona" was the uprising of the Partido Obrero de Unificacion Marxista (P.O.U.M.) and anarchist elements against the Republic. The quarrel was sufficiently nasty to prompt the I.B. headquarters to hold volunteers in France until the dissidents were put down. Barcelona was the first major city through which the Internationals passed as they came into Spain.

12. Will Paynter, a Welsh miners' leader, was not long in Spain himself, having been sent over as British Political Commissar at the I. B. headquarters in Albacete, where he served until September of 1937.

13. Malcolm Dunbar, born in Harrogate, educated at Cambridge, proved to be one of the two or three most admired British officers in the I. B. At the end, he was Chief of Staff of the XVth International Brigade. Humphrey "Hugh" Slater, a graduate of Tonbridge School, had been a peripatetic journalist on the continent. In contrast to Dunbar, he became one of the least admired officers, his affectations went before him. Sgt. John Black of Dover, died at the Battle of Brunete.

14. Miles Tomalin, a man of infinite wit, journalist and poet, survived the war to lead his comrades on the 1981 visit, tootling on the famous recorder.

15. The following international volunteers served with the British Anti-tank Battery:

Bill Alexander	Otto Estenson	Paul Pavlovski (Am.)
Jimmy Arthur	Ianto Evans	Frank Proctor
George Baker	Alan Gilchrist	Hugh Slater
?Bates	Ben Glaser	Chris Smith
Jack Black	Tom Jones	Hughie Smith
Jim Brewer	John Longdragon	Jimmy Sullivan
Eddie Brown	Jeff Mildwater	Fred Thomas
Tommy Chilvers	"Moses"	Miles Tomalin
Jim Coombs	George Murray	Andy Winter
Bill Cranston	Arthur Nicol	
?Croft	Hugh O'Hanlon	
Fraser Crombie		
Malcolm Dunbar		
John Dunlop		

16. Francisco Largo Caballero, a venerable player in Spanish politics, had been Premier of the Republic since September, 1936. The P.O.U.M crisis brought his leadership into disrepute and he gave way to Dr. Juan Negrin, his Minister of Finance, who would remain Prime Minister until the end of the war. Negrin's Minister of National Defense, Indalecio Prieto, not a friend of the

Communists, exited the cabinet in April, 1937. *Mundo Obrero* was the leading Spanish Communist Party newspaper.

17. The XVth International Brigade carried three anti-tank batteries on its table of
    organization, one British, one French and one German. Brigade headquarters
    oversaw the disposition of the batteries. Although supplied by the Soviet
    Union, the cannon used was a German model called "Rheinmetall" licensed
    for production by the Russians. It fired a 45 mm shell weighing 1.43 kg capa-
    ble of armour penetration of 38 mm from 1000 yards.

18. The Robin Hood was a pub located a few miles below Epping in Essex.

19. Fred Copeman, ex-Royal Navy and Invergordon mutineer in 1931, is an endur-
    ing legend in the British Battalion, partly because of his rough demeanor,
    because of his considerable courage, and because he went through a mighty
    change of heart about the Communist Party in the years following Spain
    which is described in his 1948 memoir, *Reason in Revolt* (London: Blandford
    Press, 1948). Most of the Battalion commissars were sent to Spain by the
    British Party. Bert Williams had been an organizer in the Midlands and a mem-
    ber of Central Committee. After Brunete, he was recalled to London.

20. The Republican Eleventh Division was commanded by Enrique Lister.

21. Jock Cunningham was one of the very earliest of the British volunteers, with
    considerable experience in the defense of Madrid in 1936 and briefly as
    Battalion commander at Jarama. He was sent home after Brunete probably
    because of the increasing evidence of severe battle stress.

22. The standard history of the British medical services in the Spanish Civil War is
    Jim Fyrth's *The Signal Was Spain*. The hospital at Huete where Fred Thomas
    was treated had as its chief surgeon, Dr. Alexander Tudor Hart. Among the
    nurses assigned there were Renee Shadbolt and Isabel Dodds, both from New
    Zealand.

23. Horner was president of the South Wales Miners Federation, from whose
    ranks had come several dozen volunteers. Jones' novel remains one of the
    great stories of the miners' struggles; its sequel, *We Live*, takes the young hero
    to his death in Spain.

24. This action was the conclusion to a three-stage campaign into the Aragon,
    launched on 24 August 1937. Three towns, Belchite, Quinto and Fuentes de
    Ebro, stood in the way of an assault on Zaragossa, a major insurgent base. One
    by one, the three obstacles were to be taken: first, Quinto, a relatively easy tar-
    get except for a foritifed hill named Purburell which the British Battalion
    stormed on the second day. Its commander, Peter Daly, fell there. Next,
    Belchite, the scene of ruinous street fighting but a victory for the XVth I. B.
    The destroyed town lies there today, a Franco monument to his dead soldiers.
    After a lull during which the Mackenzie-Papineau Battalion, newly formed of

Canadian volunteers, came forward, the Brigade moved north to Fuentes de Ebro, which it assaulted on 13 October. This attack failed completely, even though a tank squadron led the way. The Anti-tank Battery took part in all three ventures, losing one gun commander, Jim Coomes, in the streets of Belchite.

25. *Our Fight* was a Brigade newsletter published in several languages. For the historian, it is a rare and extremely useful gauge of morale.

26. The introduction of Spaniards into the international units had been assumed from the beginning. The ratio was always in flux as the months passed and the International casualties mounted while International recruits declined. Many of the battalions became dominated by Spanish ranks.

27. Pollitt made a half-dozen visits to the Battalion which were much appreciated. He maintained a regular correspondence with British political officers in Spain who looked to him for resources and for policy decisions vis a vis appointments to their own ranks and repatriation following tours of duty of the volunteers.

28. Not a few of the songs passing among the men had won their popularity in the IRA.

29. The reference is to the lifting of the siege of Mafeking in the Boer War.

30. Quiepo de Llano y Serra, at the time of his remark early in the war, commanded the Southern front in behalf of the rebellion. In an interview long afterward with the Imperial War Museum SCW project, Arthur Nicol, Political Commissar of the Battery, spoke of "two fellows in the battery . . . who had had a good education . . . who wrote little plays" one called "Franco Rides to Town." "I thought Harry [Pollitt] was going to burst his sides. . . . " IWM, 956, Arthur Nicol.

31. Hogmanay. The Scots' New Year's Eve.

32. The Two Lovers of the 15th century chose death rather than separation. Their tomb is near the Teruel Cathedral.

33. The Labor Corp might also have been called a Pioneer or Engineer unit.

34. "Major Smith" was, in fact, Edward Cecilsmith of Toronto, a journalist and self-styled adventurer. He had fought with the British Battalion at Brunete, received a wound there, returned with the Mackenzie Papineau Battalion to Fuentes de Ebro after which he assumed command on the death of Joseph Dallet, an American, who had led the unit for several weeks. The surname confused his country-men, many of whom thought he was "Cecil Smith."

35. "Alvarez del Vayo." Julio Alvarez del Vayo was Cabinet Minister under Largo Caballero and then under Negrin, as Foreign Minister. "Azana." Manuel Azana, another veteran politician, was President of the Republic on the eve of the war."Thaelmann." Ernest Thaelmann, after whom a centuria, then a battalion

and then a brigade were named, was a Hamburg stevedore and a Communist Party leader in the 1920s. Thomas would later live in the "Rosa Luxemburg" villa, named after the German radical.

36. 9 March 1938: Franco launched a five corps assault from the Aragon bound east for the Mediterranean. The XVth I. B. was recuperating in Belchite from the winter struggles in and around Teruel. Across the next weeks, Republican and International units withdrew before the "blitzkrieg," their companies and sections thrown to the winds as they struggled towards the Ebro River, a natural barrier. On 3 April, survivors of the British Battalion and the British Anti-tank Battery crossed to safety.

37. Valentin Gonzalez, whose nom de guerre was El Campesino, "the Peasant," was a division commander in the Republican Army.

38. The border with France had been re-opened in March, only to be closed again in May. Even so, sufficient munitions, petrol and other supplies had come across to enable the Republican army to give unexpected resistance to the fascists in their assault.

39. Negrin had given up on the defeatist attitude of Defense Minister Prieto and secured his resignation.

40. The BBC documentary about the veterans' return to Spain was shown in Great Britain in April, 1982.

41. William Rust wrote the first history of the British Battalion, *Britons in Spain* (London: London and Wishart, 1939). Wally Tapsell had joined the Battalion a year before; reputedly, he died assaulting an Italian armored column. Robert Merriman, an American veteran of Jarama, was believed to have been captured and then executed.

42. The Independent Labour Party had long been a factor in British labor circles, particularly in Scotland. George Orwell carried a letter of introduction from the I. L. P. when he went to Spain but did not actually join the party until after his return to England.

43. Vladimir Copic, a Yugoslav communist, had, with an occasional interruption, led the Brigade since its first days. The new commander was Jose Antonio Valledor, an Asturian miner and, by this time, a seasoned infantry officer. His appointment probably signalled the growing number of Spanish ranks.

44. A native of New York City, Wellman was a young but experienced member of the Communist Party and a busy organizer. Like Thomas, he had arrived in Spain at the time of the P.O.U.M. disturbances. Assigned to the Canadian battalion in 1937, he became its commissar after the Aragon campaigns of 1937.

45. The Mackenzie-Papineau Battalion, named for two leaders of an 1837 rebellion in Canada, was mustered into the XVth International Brigade on 1 July 1937: Dominion Day in Canada, the anniversary of Confederation.

46. Negrin's "thirteen points," issued on 1 May, were intended to rally support from the citizens and to gain credibility among international observers. There was something for everyone: belief in collective security and the League of Nations; withdrawal of all foreign troops; agrarian reform; support of small business enterprise and property liberty for all; amnesty; and perhaps most important, the resolution to continue the fight.

47. Wild had commanded the British Battalion since the Teruel campaign ex-navy, a bit of a roughneck, elemental in his nature, he remained one of the most popular and respected of the British volunteers.

48. The Captain of the Machine Gun Company was Sidney Levine, an American volunteer who had fought at Jarama.

49. The rather sour reference here is to Jason Gurney's memoir, *Crusade in Spain* (London: Faber and Faber, 1974). The South African volunteer wrote harshly of life in the British Battalion.

50. Fred Thomas eventually joined the British Army and served in India with the rank of Captain during WW II. After that, he returned to England, completed his education and became a school-master.

Index

A

Alexander, William, 160
Arthur, Jimmy, 87
Ashcroft, Peggy, 53
Atlee, Clement, 170
Azana, Manuel, 164

B

Baker, George, 8, 42-45, 50, 53, 62-63, 65, 67, 73-74, 77, 79-80, 107, 137, 140, 142
Barnardo, 107, 161
Battle of Brunete, 33-41, 71, 116
Battle of Teruel, 53-83
Battle of the Ebro, 107-60
Black, John, 18-19, 23, 37, 40, 43
Bowers, Ed, 50
British Anti-tank Battery, formation, 22-23; training on the Jarama Front, 25-32; action at Brunete, 33-41; on Thomas' return, 53; Christmas season, 1937, 55-63; action at Teruel, 65-80; on the eve of the Ebro Campaign, 107-14; attached to machine-gun company of British Battalion, 104; action in the Ebro Campaign, 115-40; Battery crew transferred to infantry, 141-43
British Battalion, 33, 35-36, 75-76, 96, 104, 112, 114, 119, 124, 126, 139, 141, 147; machine gun company, 96, 104, 110, 113, 115, 143, 149
British Broadcasting Corporation Television, 93
British Labour Party, 5, 84

C

Cannon, Karl, 85, 88
Chamberlain, Neville, 86, 123, 167
Chilvers, Tommy, 12, 19
Communist Party of Great Britain, 6-7
Cook, Jerry, 147
Cooney, Bob, 168
Copeman, Fred, 33
Copic, Vladimir, 109
Cranston, William, 62
Cripps, Sir Stafford, 170
Croft, Sergeant, 29
Cunningham, Jock, 43

D

Daily Express, 5
Daily Worker, 110
Daladier, Edouard, 167
Dependent Aid Committee, 111
Doyle, Danny, 76
Dunbar, Malcolm, 18, 23, 33-34, 36, 53-55, 62, 130, 141, 147, 163